THE ṚGVEDA

The Ṛgveda

In its Historical Setting

RAMENDRA NATH NANDI

PRIMUS BOOKS

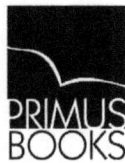

PRIMUS BOOKS

An imprint of Ratna Sagar P. Ltd.
Virat Bhavan
Mukherjee Nagar Commercial Complex
Delhi 110 009

Offices at

CHENNAI LUCKNOW
AGRA AHMEDABAD BANGALORE COIMBATORE
DEHRADUN GUWAHATI HYDERABAD JAIPUR JALANDHAR
KANPUR KOCHI KOLKATA MADURAI MUMBAI
PATNA RANCHI VARANASI

First published 2018

ISBN: 978-93-84092-89-4 (hardback)
ISBN: 978-93-84092-90-0 (POD)

Published by Primus Books

Laser typeset by Guru Typograph Technology
Crossings Republic, Ghaziabad 201 009

Printed and bound in India by Replika Press Pvt. Ltd.

Contents

Preface

THIS STUDY FOLLOWED the award of a senior academic fellowship by the Indian Council of Historical Research (ICHR) during 2005–6. Subsequently, the Council cleared the manuscript for publication and even took the initiative to this effect but could not see it through. The manuscript had to find a berth for itself with a publisher.

The work draws substantially upon a longish engagement with the life and times of old Vedic people, outlined in a monumental bardic literature. Accordingly, it deals with issues not covered elsewhere by the present writer though issues discussed in various places are touched upon here for the sake of perspective.

For text study, I have used the four-volume compendium of the *Ṛgveda* edited by F. Max Müller together with the commentary of Sāyaṇa. Text citations are in the order of book, hymn and stanza like the Fifth Book, second hymn and third stanza (5.2.3).

During the course of this investigation, I have received valuable support from a host of friends and well-wishers, particularly from the next generation.

I thank them all.

Patna R.N. NANDI

1

Introduction

THE BASIS OF the present study is a collection of 10,000-odd archaic stanzas known as the *Ṛgveda Saṃhitā*. Though Pāṇini mentions as many as six recensions of the text, only two are extant, one complete and the other fragmentary. The latter text, known as *Bāṣkalya*, may not be of much use for historical reconstruction. The *Śākalya* text which appears to have survived in full is possibly not the same as that composed thousands of years ago. The text incorporates certain events in nature and society which may have long predated the beginnings of bardic compositions, the compositions themselves being fragmentary and disjointed in nature. These compositions may have trickled down through the memory of generations of poets, who in their turn added bits to the material they inherited. Still a few centuries later, the text was taken up to produce a version in keeping with the liturgy of that time. In the process, the redactors deleted, inflated, revised and replaced certain compositions, according to their own requirements.

This is to emphasize that events taking place in the remote past, the third millennium BC in all likelihood, may not have been reproduced in situ in the text. However, whatever has survived may suffice to reconstruct the stages which may have long preceded the final redaction of the text. Since correlation of Harappan archaeology and the *Ṛgveda* compositions is no longer a matter of debate except in certain misinformed quarters, the earliest of several stages through which the people of north-western South Asia passed can be identified as the high point of a process of urbanization in the subcontinent. These times witnessed a durable interactive and interdependent system between the states that ruled the Greater Indus Valley. The states may have been five in number, each with a supreme power centre in the five megacities and each having its medium and smaller urban places. The countryside surrounding the mega-city as well as its satellite towns served as the primary basis of resource generation. The countryside comprised forests, mountains, swamps, deserts, coastal fringes besides river valleys and canals surrounded by vast agricultural land. If mathematical precision is not the focus of investigation, one can notice all these geographical features in the text. Though the text does not have a term for megacity, a good look at the description of the majestic citadels may be in order here. Consider the expressions 'massive' (*mahī*), 'broad and large' (*pṛthvī, urvī*), 'strong like metal' (*āyasī*), 'stone-built' (*aśmamayī*), 'numerous' (*bahulā*), 'many-pillared' (*sahasrasthūṇa*), 'with many gates' (*śatadura*) and 'full of resources' (*śatabhuji*) used to highlight the imposing architecture of fortified settlements (*pur*). This testifies strongly to the grandeur of Harappan cities.

Likewise, as evidence of the five states, one may point to expressions that are always prefixed by the term 'five' (*pañca*). Depending on the context, five people (*pañca jana*), five lands or states (*pañca kṣiti*), troops of five lands (*pañca śreṇī*), cultivators of five lands (*pañca caraṣaṇī*), and cultures of five lands (*pañca kṛṣṭi*). The use of these expressions in the *Ṛgveda*, however, is rather indiscriminate. The expression *pañca hotṛn* may relate to five different segments of bards and priests, each belonging to one or the other of five lands (*pañca kṣiti*). This high point of urbanization was followed by a downturn in all sectors of production, agriculture, trade and crafts following large-scale depredations in nature, which affected social harmony, leading to unrest, a quest for new resources and violent conflicts. The results were predictable and the bards record these accordingly. The lesser availability of basic resources like food led to malnutrition, disease, hunger and deaths from starvation.[1] Given this scenario, the end of urbanization would have been inevitable; this, too, was well recorded by the poets.

This context may also help to understand the very basis of *Ṛgveda* compositions. The term *Ṛgveda* means knowledge (from √*vid*, 'to know') or knowledge text of prayers (√*ṛk*). But prayers to whom and why? A close look at the context reveals that everything that mattered in the life of the people, good or bad, was invoked, the benign for protection and well being and the malign to guard against any malefic influence. Briefly, this sums up the very ethos of an ideology of nature worship. The term 'nature' needs to be understood in its widest sense—the sun, moon, stars, sky, earth, dawn, dusk, night, winds, rains, storm winds, cosmic energy, high seas, rivers, mountains, trees, forests, birds, and animals. Prayers are also recited to ward off the goddess of death (*nirṛti*), disease, hunger, starvation, malnutrition, and famines.

Agriculture

Since agriculture formed the basis of everything in society, the peasant is praised just as the land he cultivates, the bulls that draw the plough, the furrows that the plough creates, the different parts of the plough, the man who ploughs and, of course, the landowner or the god of cultivable land. The mention of *kṣetravid* and *kṣetrasādhas* signifies the importance of soil testing and measurement of land into plots. A distinction is made between fertile plough lands (*urvarā*) and infertile land (*khila*). Besides, there are other terms like *bhūmi, kṣetra, dāna* and *pṛthvī* which, too, depending on the context, signify cultivable land. Prayers were offered to different divinities, particularly Indra, Agni and Aśvins, to provide the Aryas with plentiful fertile land.

The produce of the land included all varieties of grain, pulses, seeds, besides sugarcane. As for the summer crops, the presence of rice is already well documented in archaeology, from about the beginning of the second millennium BC.[2] There is also good archaeological documentation of wheat, barley, all types of millets, pulses and oil seeds. Generic terms like *dhānya, yava* and *sasa* covered all these products of the field. We come across terms like *Dhānyakṛta*, or grain cultivator, and *Dhānyaṃ Bījaṃ Akṣitam*, i.e. well-processed grain seeds preserved for the next season. The mention of grain stores (*urdaraṃ, sthivi*) signifies the surplus orientation of peasant production. The term *odan* also signifies consumption of grain, probably rice. At one place mention is made of *kṣīrapāk odanam* or rice boiled with milk, which is widely-consumed in large parts of India with or without a little sweetener. Consumption of cereals is well testified by frequent references to offerings of cereal dishes to the divinities (3.52.1–7). Ground grain was used to make different types of cake—baked, lightly fried or deep fried. *Puroḍāsa*, a hard, baked or lightly fried cake, probably the *Ṛgvedic* precursor of *pārātha*, is widely consumed in large parts of India even today. Grain powder or flour (*saktu*) and parched grain (*dhānā*) were other favourite dishes of the divinities. A gruel consisting of grain flour and curd was offered to the toothless god Puṣan. Another favourite dish was the deep-fried cake (*apūpa*), the *Ṛgvedic* predecessor of *puā*, also relished in large parts of India.

Agriculture also included the cultivation of pulses and oil seeds and the production of jaggery or sugar. The paucity or absence of separate terms for pulses, oil seeds and jaggery need not suggest their absence from the fields of *Ṛgvedic* peasants, who shared the same geographical space and timeline with the Harappans. Crops once produced in a particular geographical area become permanent culinary items there, even spreading to adjoining regions. The later *Saṃhitā* texts—*Atharvaveda, Sāmaveda,* and *Yajurveda*—which may have been developing incipiently alongside the *Ṛgveda*, continued to expand as disorder in nature and society intensified about the close of the third millennium BC. The inflation of rituals, ostensibly intended to contain disorders in nature and society but substantially aimed at increasing the priestly coffers, took place between 1900 and 1500 BC. In these texts, separate terms are mentioned for pulses, oil seeds and jaggery. As for the *Ṛgveda*, terms like *dhānya, yava* and *sasa* may have included all varieties of grains, including pulses. As for oil seeds and jaggery, the people mentioned in the *Ṛgveda* would not have denied themselves the luxury of oil seeds and jaggery enjoyed by their contemporary Harappans.

Turning to the Harappan evidence during the third millennium BC, one has to fall back on archaeo-botanical studies which substantially illuminate the horizons of our information. According to a study by Fuller, all varieties of pulses—West Asian, African and Indian—have been encountered at Miriqalat on the Indo-Iranian border in a fourth millennium BC context.[3] The study also shows that most Harappan sites in Pakistan produced only winter pulses whereas those on the Indian side produced both winter and summer pulses.[4] Those variations may have been because of the annual precipitation. Interestingly, the Harappans, or more appropriately, the Vedic Harappans, consumed all varieties of pulses which the South Asian relish today, regional preferences notwithstanding. The pulses include black gram (*urad*), red gram (*arhar*), green gram (*mung*), lentil (*masur*), horse gram (*kulthi*), bengal gram (*chana*), grass pea (*kesari*), pea (*matar*), bonavist bean (*sem*), moth bean (*moth*), cow pea (*chowli*) and a few more.[5]

As for the oils, the Harappans produced brown mustard (*Brassica Junsica*, *Rai*), sesame (*til*), linseed (*tisi*) and castor (*errand*). Cotton seeds also provided a good source of cooking oil.[6] The first three were surely used as edible oils but castor oil was used for lighting purposes. Cottonseed oil, which has great nutritional value, is also considered to be a good cooking medium, particularly for deep frying, baking and making salads. Dates which grew aplenty in the area were also a source of edible oil.[7] Though there is no evidence forthcoming so far, dry coconuts or copra may also have been an important source of edible oil.

As for jaggery or raw sugar, the principal source was sugarcane, which first grew in the wild but was later on domesticated for market production. The discovery of date stones from various Harappan sites surely suggests that the date and date palm juice were other important sources of jaggery. Date palm juice, when fermented, can also be consumed as country liquor as South Asians do today in the countryside.

A diligent investigator of the text will notice elaborate but scattered information relating to different forms of irrigation. Six seasons are mentioned and the summer precipitation was eagerly awaited by the peasants. The Frog Hymn of the text shows how the ponds and reservoirs became dry during high summer and the frogs hiding inside the soil started croaking as the monsoon (*prāvṛt*) set in. Besides two annual precepitations, peasants used both drift irrigation and lift irrigation, the former through channels (*khanitrimā*) connected with rivers and other water bodies and the latter with the help of pulley and suction. Pulley was used in the case of large, deep wells and suction in the case of masonry underground channels which ran for long distances, and water tapped wherever needed. At Dholavira in Kutch, masonry underground channels were constructed to tap and preserve rain water in reservoirs, both inside and outside the city. This conservation of water was meant for the lean season.

As things deteriorated in the wake of widespread geo-climatic disorders, there were conflicts for control of water bodies, sometimes leading to destruction of bunds and barrages. Though the individual land holdings were demarcated fairly well, encroachments by adjacent landholders frequently led to violent brawls like it has always happened in South Asian villages. Frequent allusions to fights undertaken to capture fertile agricultural land in neighbourhood villages, demarcation of the new land into plots and distribution of these plots among stakeholders together with the harvest may, however, underline the stressful times towards the sunset years of urbanization.

Trade and Crafts

A market economy of towns thrives on surplus production in all sectors of human consumption. Though there is no term meaning 'market' in the text, all activities connected with a market system are mentioned. Goods were sold and purchased, and unfair trade practices like substandard and underweight commodities were resented. The trader was known to be a habitually crafty person (*vaṇik vanku*). Though not explicitly mentioned, the trading community seems to have been divided according to the category of production managed by each group. There are long descriptions, though scattered, of long distance trade, both overland and overseas, the former by means of caravans and the latter using a fleet of ships. Depending on the terrain, the caravaneers employed bullocks, camels, ponies or mules and even horses to draw the carts laden with merchandise. Separate carts were used to carry the goods and the caravaneers who included traders, cooks, attendants, armed escorts and other staff. The poets frequently refer to ambushes by wayside marauders who bargained hard to appropriate as much of the goods as they could in order to let the group move forward. As for the overseas trade, large boats were employed to carry the men and material as in the case of caravans. Maritime trade was also fraught with dangers like shipwrecks, loss of direction and piracy. One shipwreck incident is described in great detail by the poets. The ships were also capable of launching rescue operations in any such eventuality. The Aśvins who appear in different roles in different portions of the text, sometimes as navigators and at other times as physicians and surgeons, are said to have had their home on the high seas. The threat of piracy was negotiated by tactfully handling the pirates, by giving as little of the merchandise as the traders were willing to spare. In the event of loss of direction, the flight course of seafaring birds proved helpful.

As for the goods produced and marketed, these came from several areas: fields, pastures, hills, forests, marshlands, deserts and coastal colonies. Mines provided precious metals and gemstones. The metals included gold (*hiraṇya*), bronze and brass (*hiraṇya saṃdṛśa*) and probably silver (*candra*). Iron was already known in the third millennium BC, judging by the discovery of iron objects at Mohenjo-daro in Sind and Mundigak in Afghanistan. Mining is mentioned, though in a typically elliptical manner, in which the poets furnish the relevant information. 'The mouth of the mine was opened like eggs of birds are opened' (10.68.7). There is an interesting simile which relates to precious materials extracted from the mines like 'one sucks out the marrow of a bone' (10.68.9). The mined goods were then transported in carts drawn by bullocks, camels and horses to the processing unit. The merchants may have procured the finished goods in bulk from these units.

Craft goods of diverse descriptions constitute the baseline of human habitations everywhere—cities, villages, forests, hills, deserts, coastal areas and marshlands. For an urban system, these goods are needed in large quantities. Scanning the text, one comes across specialized groups producing different types of craft goods. The smith (*karmāra*) and the smelter (*dhmātā*) are mentioned. Since both required specialized skills, it is unlikely that the two were combined in the same hands. As for the metals, gold, copper, alloys of copper (bronze and brass), iron and probably silver were known. The carpenter occupied an important place in the old Vedic society. The term denoting 'carpenter' is *takṣa*, which occurs only once in the text. But this is more than compensated by five sizeable hymns of the Fourth Book which raised the four carpenter brothers, headed by Ṛbhu, to the position of divinity, who were entitled to a share of the evening oblations (*tṛtīye sāve*) and frequently praised as the givers of wealth (*ratnadheyī*). The term *ratnadheyī* may signify the carpenters' skills in making carts, boats and ships, all fetching and ferrying every kind of valuable commodity.

The weaver (*vāsovāya, vayantī*) was another important member of the community of craftsmen. Weaving seems to have been a household craft. But the gifts of ten types of cloths or bards carrying large bundles of textiles, the latter surely a textile trader who could also compose stanzas in praise of the donor king, suggest large-scale production of different types of textiles. This would be possible only if the craft was pursued in several workshops, domestic or otherwise. The weaving over, the clothes were washed, well-dried and dyed in different hues. Details of different parts of the weaving apparatus are mentioned. Mention is also made of two women crossing one another in the process of weaving.

The gift of ten types of cloth (6.47.23) provides a fair indication of the extensive and diverse nature of the textile industry. Some idea of this diversity is provided by archaeo-botanical studies on the subject. There were several different plant sources that provided fibres for making as many kinds of cloths. These sources included cotton, jute and flax (*Linum usitatissimum*, *tisi*). Since the prehistoric Indus Valley is said to be the birthplace of cotton, the popularity of cotton cloths in the whole area does not need to be emphasized. Cotton fibres have been identified at Mehargarh in a sixth millennium BC context whereas charred cotton seeds have been reported in a fifth millennium BC context also at Mehargarh. Flax has been identified at Miriqalat in a fourth millennium BC context.[8] In addition to these, silk was also used for cloths. The silk industry of the prehistoric Indus Valley developed independently with the help of indigenous techniques, the chief source being wild silk moth.[9] A fifth important source of clothing was wool which was produced in large quantities during the Harappan period. Like woollens, leather was also used for winter wear. For textual support, one may turn to a stanza in praise of the river Indus (10.75.8) which describes it as *Suvāsā, Sīlamavatī* and *Urṇāvatī*. *Suvāsā* may represent cotton cloth, while *Sīlamavatī* may relate to jute and flax. The term *Urṇāvatī* may be a fair representation of both silk and wool.

Leather workers are also alluded to, though in a confusing manner. The term is *carmamnā*, meaning a mind centred on leather. However one does not have to rely too much on this vocable in view of details surfacing on different aspects of leather production. The process of tanning is evident from the reference to hides dipped in tank water. Mention is also made of a king who gave away a large bundle of different kinds of leather to a bard, who may have been a leather merchant as well. The importance of hides can also be seen from diverse uses to which leather was put like preparing bows, fixing different parts of a chariot, making of musical instruments, manufacture of boats and ships besides garments of different types. The presence of other artisans like goldsmith is also evident from the mention of ornaments made from gold like the gold earrings (*hiraṇya karṇa*) and gold necklaces (*niṣka grīva*) besides necklaces made from gems (*maṇi grīva*).

The Political System

On the political horizon, the state seems to have taken firm roots. Monarchy, dynastic or elective, was the general rule but going by the term *Janarājñaḥ* or tribal kings, tribal states are also mentioned. The political terminology which is quite impressive includes the terms *rājya* (kingdom), *rāṣṭra* (realm, dominion, country), *rājā* (king), *rājñī* (queen), *rājakā* (minor kings), *rājaputra* (prince), *samrāṭ* (emperor), *samrājñī* (empress), *rājanya* (royal associates), *kṣatra* (power, supremacy), *kṣatriya* (powerful, endowed with sovereignty), *dūta* (messenger), *senānī* (commander) and *grāmaṇī* (village headman). The king lived in fortified palaces with bards singing in his honour every morning. The chief priest was the chief adviser while the queen (*mahiṣī*) figured quite high in the administrative structure. The *rājanya* or the fellow associates also formed an important rung in the royal administration. The *senānī* was the commander of the armed forces while the *grāmaṇī* was the chief representative of the king in the countryside. The messenger or *dūta* was the chief communicator between chiefs of different states as well as between the king and the people. The kingdom is said to have frontiers on all the four sides—east, west, north, south, besides a central region. The role of corporate bodies in the administration is underlined. There was a general assembly called *sabhā* which comprised important persons of the state besides certain representatives of the king to function as the connection between the king and the assembly. The other body was the *samiti* which comprised important officers and ministers of the king. This was a small body and appears to have functioned as the cabinet of the king. The quest for sovereign power (*kṣatra*) is frequently mentioned and armed expeditions were undertaken to extend the territory of the king through conquest.

The ritual of the *Aśvamedh* sacrifice is addressed at length in two consecutive hymns (1.162, 1.163). The term *Aśvamedh* figures thrice as the name of a king elsewhere in the text. There is no mention of the term in these two hymns though details of the sacrifice are mentioned. Scanning the two hymns, one learns that a chosen horse was sanctified and decorated appropriately as the representative of the king with a flag hoisted on its back and ceremonially set free together with a group of warriors, and carts carrying the commissariat, cooks, attendants and other menials. Unaware of its mission, the sacrificial horse frequently strayed away from its track and had to be retrieved. There is no mention of what happened when the horse landed in another chief's territory. Maybe some were befriended and some others subjugated. On its return, the horse was taken to a designated area where priests, members of the royalty and other dignitaries took their respective seats. The horse was given a ceremonial bath, decorated appropriately, fed well and then taken to the place of slaughter. The legs were tied and the slaughterer decapitated the horse with the help of his associates. Different parts of the horse designated to be offered to various divinities were carefully cleaned and presented to them. The meat was then cooked in a large cauldron, with the cook removing the lid several times to check the quality of cooking and quickly replacing it to prevent any loss of flavour. When ready, the cooked meat was served to the gathering in keeping with the status of individuals and groups. Chants were recited aloud, supposedly to enable the king to imbibe the prowess of the victorious horse (now despatched to the divinities) to acquire supreme authority (*kṣatra*), presumably over the entire territory negotiated by the horse during its journey.

The Liturgy

As for the liturgy, it was already well-developed in the text. As the focus of the priesthood shifted from the word 'oblation' (*kavya havya*) to elaborate fire rituals, the sacerdotal community which started with just one priest, the *Adhvaryu*, literally the one going to or occupying the place of sacrifice (*adhvar*), for performing all the different jobs, with or without assistants, one comes across as many as seven different categories of priests, each occupied with a single job. These ranks were *Hotā* (the inviter), *Potā* (the Purifier), *Praśāstā* (the administrator), *Agnidh* (the fireman), *Neṣṭā* (the harbinger), *Udgātā* (the melodyman) and *Brahmā* whose precise functions are not clear. Add to this the calendar man or *Ṛtvij* who determined appropriate months and days for different types of sacrifice. Already in the text, one hears of a sacrifice continuing throughout the year (*Sāmvatsara*).

A metrical study of the concerned hymns already shows the emergence of metres like *Triṣṭubh*, *Jagatī*, *Bṛhatī*, *Anuṣṭubh* and *Pankti*. According to Arnold,[10] the text also contains later varieties of *Anuṣṭubh* and *Pankti* which he describes as epic *Anuṣṭubh* and epic *Pankti*. Here it is worthwhile to mention that the text compositions can be divided into several segments, the more important and sizeable of which are the liturgical *Ṛgveda* and the popular *Ṛgveda*.[11] The compositions of the popular *Ṛgveda* did not have much to do with liturgy whereas the liturgical *Ṛgveda* is obsessed with the ritual aspect. Such compositions go by the name of hymns, which are all poems though all poems in the text are not hymns.[12]

The splintering and multiplication of priestly groups because of professional competition, exclusive identity and surplus sharing, fuelled the composition of the later *Saṃhitā* texts—the *Sāma*, the *Yajus*, the *Atharvan*. The *Sāmaveda* seems to have been the exclusive domain of chantsmen and singers at the sacrifice. The *Yajurveda*, on the other hand, became the exclusive domain of fire ritualists. Quite different from this, the *Atharvaveda* seems to have been the exclusive document of the occultists and the medicine men. Already in the *Ṛgveda,* there is fair indication of the rivalry between the occultists, pejoratively described as *yātumatī*, meaning the occult-minded. But when divinities like Indra themselves performed such magic, it is appreciatively described as *māyā*. As for the conflict between the *Atharvan* healers and Indra, mention may be made of Dadhīchi who possessed secret knowledge of medicine and surgery and was eliminated by Indra on refusal to divulge this knowledge. For further splintering of each of these groups, one may turn to the large number of *Brāhmaṇa* texts, which may not have been too far removed from the timeline of the three later *Saṃhitā* texts. Such inflation of the liturgy and the priestly community could not have happened without substantial social churning, leading to the emergence of small *Janapada* states, and resource generation, with the king or the chief calling the shots.

Normally the liturgy consisted of a few prayers to please or placate whatever was around between the sky and the earth. Since the prayers had to be recited in the liturgical dialect, patronizing a bard could do the miracle for the newly initiated. This done, the newcomer could rightfully describe himself as Arya or Noble people. Ethnicity, language and lifestyle did not come in the way of this. Two good examples are Divodāsa and Sudāsa, originally non-Aryan *Dāsa* chiefs, who after embracing the new faith became legendary kings and patrons of the Arya. A paktha or pakhtoon chief figures prominently in several *dānastuti* hymns of the Eighth Book. In the Tenth Book, Sibi Auśīnara, probably a native of the Sibi region, figures as the composer of an entire hymn.

The Geographical Limits

The bardic compositions relate to a vast geographical area, stretching from Haryana, Rajasthan and Gujarat in the east to Baluchistan, Afghanistan and parts of eastern Iran in the west; from the south-central Asian borderlands, the Swat Valley and the Kashmir Valley in the north to the Rann of Kutch and Sind in the south. Evidence of this comes from various categories of sources already embedded in the text—the hydronyms, the ethnonyms and the description of the high seas. The names of the more important rivers which can be deduced from the hydronyms are the Yamunā, the Sarasvatī, the Vyasa (Beas), the Sutlej, the Ravi, the Chenab, the Indus, the Swat, the Kabul, the upper reaches of the Oxus (Skt. *Vakṣu* but Aṃśumatī in the text), the western Sarasvatī (Avestan, Haraxvaity; old Persian, Harauti; modern, Argandab), the Sarayu (old Persian, Haroiva; Greek, Aria), the Gomatī (modern Gomal), the Kubha (Kabul), the Krumu (Kurram), the Havyāvatī (Zhob), and the Bolan Valley suggested by the ethnonym *Bhalanas*. The ethnonyms come for an asking. The more important of these are the Pakthas, the Alinas, the Śivas, the Bhalanas, the Parsava, the Parthava, the Ajas, the *Śigrus*, the *Yakṣus*, the *Gāndhāris* and many others. It is difficult to identify all the ethnic groups at the present state of our knowledge. But some identifications are not difficult, like Pakhtoons (Pakthas), Sibis (Śivas) or inhabitants of the Sibi region in Pakistan, Bolanese (Bhalanas), the horn-hooded Śakas (*viṣāṇin, śṛngin*, probably horn-hooded *śaka tigrekhuda* of the old Persian inscriptions), Persians (Parsava), the Parthians (Parthva), inhabitants of the Sikar region of Rajasthan (Śigru), the people of Ajnala region of Amritsar district (Ajas) and probably an ethnic group coming from the upper Oxus Valley (Yakṣu). The Gāndhāris may have inhabited the Gāndhāra region.

The identification of the Valley of Kashmir depends on three crucial topographical features. The term *Udavraja* (floating pastures) relates to rafters with a cover of soil and crops grown on these floating rafters. Second, the lone allusion to a north-flowing course of the river Indus (*Sodañcaṃ sindhuṃ*), which appears in connection with the episode of Śambara and his pit dwellings. The only point where the river Indus turns due north is some distance from Skardu in the Gilgit Baltistan region. After flowing nearly 25 km. northwards, the river turns due south and after covering some distance finally takes a south-western trajectory. The third qualifier relates to the hundred forts (*pur*) of Śambara which Indra destroyed, one of which he retained for his own use. The archaeological excavations conducted in the Karewa mud basin of the Jhelum Valley confirm the existence of pit dwellings which can be dated between 2500 and 1200 BC. The interconnected pit dwellings with just a few distant openings may have appeared to concerned bards as being invincible and hence the term *pur*. This, it would appear, had more to do with the poet's desire to hype the exemplary strength of his patron just like he attributed the northward flow of the Indus to the superhuman strength of Indra.

The Rann of Kutch is fairly well represented by the term *Iriṇa*, which makes several appearances and the descriptions coincide with the present condition of the Rann. The term

'Śaryāṇāvat' (8.6.39, 8.7.29) may relate to the land of reeds and the name of a lake in Kurukṣetra. Accordingly, the poets may be referring to modern Haryana or a part of it. The place name 'Harappa', which also designates the Indus Valley civilization, already appears in the text in connection with a fight between a Parthian chief and his South Asian detractor who is said to have been eliminated on the eastern flank of Harappa (*hariyuppiyāyām hanpūrve*, 6.27.5).

The aforementioned observations are far too inadeqate to provide even a cursory outline of the information recorded in the text. This may be even beyond the scope of a comprehensive monograph. It would suffice, however, if the readers get a feel of the events taking place in nature and society and the milieu in which the poets were operating. In case the Harappan chronology undergoes a drastic upward revision as suggested in a recent study by Sarkar et al.,[13] the Vedic chronology may have to be suitably revised with mid-fourth or late-fourth millennium BC as the take-off time, the parameters of the text and archaeology correlation remaining unaffected. The findings of this new study have been very briefly summarized later on in Chapter 6. However, its results may call for much more precision relating to millennial chrono-zones, both inter-millennial and intra-millennial, to be determined on the basis of climate, habitational remains and lifestyles in different parts of the Harappan civilizational area. Besides, similar evidence from other Harappan sites would also be required.

Notes

1. R.N. Nandi, *Ideology and Environment: Situating the Origin of Vedic Culture*, Delhi: Akaar, 2009, chapter 7.

2. H. Fujiwara, M.R. Mughal, A. Sasaki, and T. Matano, 'Rice and Ragi at Harappa: Preliminary Results by Plant Opal Analysis', *Pakistan Archaeology*, vol. 27, 1992, pp. 129–42, 369–80; repr., in *The Decline and Fall of the Indus Civilization*, ed. N. Lahiri, New Delhi: Permanent Black, 2000.
3. D.Q. Fuller and E.C. Harvey, 'The Archaeobotany of Indian Pulses: Identification, Processing and Evidence for Cultivation', *Environmental Archaeology*, vol. 11, no. 2, 2006, pp. 219–46.
4. Ibid., p. 221.
5. Ibid., p. 220.
6. J.R. McIntosh, *The Ancient Indus Valley: New Perspectives*, Santa Barbara, California: ABC-CLIO, 2008, chapter 5, p. 114.
7. Ibid.
8. R.P. Wright, D.L. Lentz, H.F. Beaubien and C.K. Kimbrough, 'New Evidence for Jute (*Corchorus Capsularis L.*) in the Indus Civilization', *Archaeological and Anthropological Sciences*, vol. 4, no. 2, 2012, pp. 137–43.
9. I.L. Good, J.M. Kenoyer and R.H. Meadow, 'New Evidence for Early Silk in the Indus Civilization', *Archaeometry*, vol. 51, no. 3, 2009, pp. 457–66.
10. E.V. Arnold, *Vedic Metre in its Historical Development*, 1st edn., Cambridge: Cambridge University Press, 1905; repr., Delhi: Motilal Banarsidass, 1967, pp. 1, 21.
11. Ibid.
12. Ibid.
13. A. Sarkar, A.D. Mukherjee, M.K. Bera, B. Das, N. Juyal, P. Morthekai, R.D. Deshpande, V.S. Shinde and L.S. Rao, 'Oxygen Isotope in Archaeological Bioapatities from India: Implications to Climate Change and Decline of Bronze Age Harappan Civilization', *Nature.com*, Scientific Reports 6, no. 26555, 2016.

2
Timing the Text

THE DATING OF the *Ṛgveda* has to proceed either on the basis of paleo-linguistic stratification of the text or on the basis of the correspondence of internal evidence with known archaeological contexts in north-western South Asia during the Bronze Age. A third basis suggested by certain linguists is the internal sequence of royal dynasties and political events outlined in the text.[1] The latter has led to an upward revision of the *Ṛgvedic* chronology by nearly 250 years. Accordingly, the *Ṛgveda* turns out to be a Bronze-Age (pre-Iron-Age) text of the Greater Punjab that followed the dissolution of the Indus Civilization. However, in the absence of firmly dated historical events, Witzel's revised chronology does not make much headway except making the text coterminous with the closing stages of

Harappan urbanization (1900–1700 BC). Witzel's attempt to limit the geographical expanse of the text to the Punjab is already flawed since the textual evidence, as we have seen earlier, shows that the spread of the bardic composers was far and wide.

Probably, the whole problem of dating needs a reconsideration, which can be attempted either on the basis of internal stratification or on the basis of correlation of textual material with some firmly established historical developments or a combination of both. The former exercise, based only on linguistic considerations, will surely lay bare the stages of phonological, lexical or structural changes within each of these texts. For instance, in relation to the Old Avesta, scholars have identified as many as five stages of the language.[2] There is, however, little possibility of ascertaining from this what particular historical developments, in which periods, influenced these changes. On the contrary, it is quite likely that information contained in different portions of the texts do not have any relation with the linguistic stages with which they are associated by scholars. Some of the materials may even predate the earliest portions of the texts by a considerable period of time, as in the case of the Avestan fire cult of Atas-Zohr, which is said to go back at least to the third millennium BC.[3] This realization is occasionally reflected in certain writings though it has not been put to good use, methodologically, for historical reconstruction.

Third Millennium BC: The Take-off Time

In relation to the *Ṛgveda*, there has been no attempt so far, perhaps none is possible either, to stratify the text on the basis of linguistic features. As for the correlation of textual data with historical developments, one must begin with the understanding that there is no organic chronological relationship between these literary compositions and the information they contain.

To begin with, one may envisage three chronological layers, each separated from the other by several centuries. The first in this order would be the time or times which are witness to certain historical events in nature and society. The next in the order would be the time when information about these began to surface in some of the bardic compositions. The third, much later, stage would relate to the time when these compositions were edited and compiled into a ritual text more than once and by different groups of priests, each group deleting, inflating, revising and replacing certain compositions, according to their own requirements. It is to the earliest of these stages that we are addressing our discourse. The developments, underlined on the basis of the correlation of textual and archaeological evidence, include the Fire cult, the Sun-cult, the funerary practices, the Soma-cult, and the three phases of urbanization in the Greater Indus Valley—mature, degenerate and deserted.

From Chants to Fire Rituals

An exercise in relation to the stages of liturgical development contained in the text may be worthwhile and is likely to throw up certain known historical contexts. Examining the bardic passages closely, one might come to the conclusion that the ideology of *Daiva* worship evolved in phases. At the earliest stage, chants alone sufficed to communicate with the divinities. The chants comprised short and cryptic sentences. These chants also served as an oblation to the gods. Over time, the need for more elaborate and placatory invocations was felt. Accordingly, different types of similes or metaphors were added to these cryptic sentences, and with a permutation of phonemes, mantras began to take different metrical shapes. Even in the present text, there are hundreds of invocations, which implore the divinities to be satisfied with the ecstatic recitation of chants though no objects of offering are mentioned. The absence of accent marks in a large number of these passages seems to suggest the uncertainty of metrical form, each composition adopting various forms in different priestly contexts.

Priests began to associate fire with the chants only subsequently, following their belief that the smoke could act as a carrier of prayer-offerings to concerned divinities. Here one must distinguish between the prayers directly addressed to the Fire God, just like to other divinities, and the invocation of ritualistic fire as the mediator between the gods and those making the oblation. It was the latter belief that gave rise to the practice of offering food and drink to the fire, in order to be conveyed to the various divinities.

The fire cult is already well-documented in the Harappan archaeology of mid-third millennium BC, though the practice was not uniform everywhere.[4] At Kalibangan, we have firepits built on brick platforms with evidence of animal sacrifice. At Harappa or Mohenjo-daro, however, no such material has been excavated. Representations on seals and sealings discovered from Harappa nevertheless indicate the practice of carrying the fire-holds in a ceremonial procession.[5] At Mohenjo-daro, some scholars have tried to identify a certain structure as a fire temple.[6] Of the three types of fire worship, the one at Kalibangan seems to be the most closely related to the *Ṛgvedic* fire cult. During the second millennium BC, the structural evidence of the fire cult has been noticed by certain archaeologists within the Bactria-Margiana archaeological complex.[7] This may have resulted from the diffusion of Harappan influences, which are well-documented in south Turkmenistan sites like Altyn-depe during the mid-third millennium BC.[8]

In the *Ṛgveda*, Angirāses and Bhṛgus are recognized as the pioneers of the fire cult. The term *angirā* itself is derived from *angārā* or charcoal fire of which there is good evidence in the fire-pits of Kalibangan. On the other hand, the Bhṛgus are repeatedly praised as the people who brought the fire out of its hiding place (*guhāhitam*) and established it among the people. In all likelihood, this signifies the post-urban Harappan practice of consecrating the ritual community fire in the open ground instead of fire-pits built of bricks, as at Kalibangan, which following the decline of urban places was no longer possible. In the *Ṛgveda*, there is no reference to any of the three sacrificial fires, the Gārhyapatya, the Āhavanīya and the Dakṣiṇāgni, though the frequent description of the domestic fire as the chief of the household (*gṛhpati*) may not leave much doubt about the ritual sanctity of the hearth's fire. In the Avestan context, the sanctity of the hearth's fire is said to go back to the third millennium BC. In comparison, there are numerous references to the Vidatha folk assembly, the activities of which were centred on a community sacrificial fire, representing a system of a public fire cult. However, as already stated, the development need not really coincide with the fire cult of mid-third millennium BC. If at all, this may signify a tradition of public fire cults remembered by the remote descendants of urban Harappans during the post-urban phase and incorporated into their liturgical kit.

The open-ground Vidatha sacrificial fire, which figures repeatedly in the *Ṛgveda*, and which was meant for the entire community rather than individual households, may appear significant in this context. The term vedi, meaning 'a fire altar', which became commonplace during the later Vedic period, understandably occurs extremely rarely in the text.

The Cult of the Solar Disc

The importance of the Sun God in the *Ṛgveda* can be seen from the large number of divinities, five male and two female, associated with the solar pantheon. Numerically, the compositions addressed to these divinities may still be far fewer than those addressed to Indra, Agni or Soma. But the divinities of the solar galaxy were of a much more primordial nature and organically related to life-cycles than any other divinity. The cultic importance of the solar disc is also too obvious to be emphasized. In archaeological terms, the earliest documentation of this solar disc comes from the Harappan area during the mid-third millennium BC in the form of the Swastika symbol. About the same time, the Swastika forms part of Harappan ideas and materials at the proto-urban site of Altyn-depe in south Turkmenistan. Towards the close of the second millennium BC, the Swastika appears at Tahirbay-3 in the lower Murghab delta and is attributed to the southward diffusion of Andronovo culture during the second half of the second millennium BC.[9] But the Tahirbay Swastika can also be attributed to the north-easterly diffusion of south Turkmenistan cultures along the Murghab River during the early and mid-second millennium BC. The decline of the Early Bronze Age civilization may also account for the movement of certain Indo-Iranian people into south-eastern Europe, where the Kurgan builders of late third and early second millennium BC have left sufficient indication of the cultic solar disc in the form of circles, concentric circles and radiating circles.[10] The cult of the solar disc also found its way into Egypt through Harappan-Egyptian interactions during the sixteenth and fifteenth centuries BC. However, it needs to be emphasized that the worship of the Sun God in Egypt and Mesopotamia is as old as the Harappan civilization of early and mid-third millennium BC, but the significance of the solar disc as an object of worship seems to be exclusive to the Harappans and their successors. However, the cult of the solar disc patronized by Akhenaten, one of the last kings of the Egyptian eighteenth dynasty, around late fifteenth century BC may have something to do with the dispersal of Vedic-speaking Aryans in all directions following the catastrophic geo-climatic events of the Middle Bronze Age.

The Urban Context

The objection against any likening of the Harappans with the Aryas of the *Ṛgveda* does not cut much ice. For obvious textual reasons, any objective investigator will notice three different strands in the bardic description of urban places. First, there are passages that extoll the virtues of life, its security and prosperity within the four walls of the citadels. To this genre of verses, we may add passages that describe the three most important divinities of the *Ṛgvedic* pantheon—Indra (8.69.8), Agni (6.2.7) and Soma (9.107.10)—as chiefs ruling from their citadels. Indra is already a chief *par excellence,* who used to be praised like people praise the citadel (*dhṛṣṇu puraṃ na arcat*). Agni is the lord of the sacrifice and sits at the place of sacrifice like a king in a citadel. Soma on the other hand is the lord of Soma sacrifice who sits inside the Soma pot like a king sits in a citadel. Other divinities associated with the citadels are Marūts (1.166.8) and Sarasvatī (7.95.1). Poets at all times and in all countries relate to icons of their contemporary life and likewise are the comparisons made by the Vedic poets. The iconic importance of fortified settlements is also evident from the description of the citadels, mentioned previously in Chapter 1. All of this fits exactly with what the Harappan citadels looked like during the mature urban phase.

The more recurring theme of the bardic compositions, however, relates to the politics of space, involving neighbouring chiefs who were trying to extend their hegemonic control over citadels in the vicinity. The citadels were frequently captured together with vast cultivable land and water bodies lying outside them. This clearly signals a social upheaval caused by inadequate production and accumulation of resources in the wake of persistent geo-climatic disorders like low precipitation, reduced annual recharge of rivers, tectonic lifts causing dislocation of river channels, earthquakes and civil war. Besides, the confusion was worsened by marine regression, causing dislocation of sea ports, and the decline of maritime trade. Needless to say, that overland trade routes had already become unsafe, considerably reducing the flow of caravan traffic on these routes.[11]

The third category of information relates to a period when urban settlements had completely collapsed and the citadels were in complete ruins or extremely decrepit, like the condition in which they are found even today.

Clearly, the *Ṛgveda* is witness to the three well-known stages of urban life of north-western South Asia, namely, the mature urban phase (2600–2400 BC), the degenerate urban phase (2400–2000 BC), and the post-urban phase (2000–1700 BC). These stages are fairly well-represented in the Harappan archaeology of the mainland. In the Saurashtra and Kathiawar regions, however, the mature phase ranged from 2200 to 2000 BC while the decaying phase ranged from 1900 to 1700 BC.

In the Harappan context, the town is almost invariably represented by a fortified area, whether it is a citadel, a middle-town, downtown or religious complex. Jostling crowds in busy marketplaces, networks of roads and drains and buildings of different types of architectural features were all found inside the fortification. The few terms that the bards used to describe these places were *pur*, *vṛtra* and *durga* for strongholds and *armaka* or *vailasthāna* for ruined settlements. In the absence of a satisfactory Indo-Aryan derivation, the term *pur* may have been a bardic form of the Dravidian *ur* meaning a village or town. However, the bardic descriptions always represent the *pur* as a stronghold invariably belonging to the resourceful in all segments of the population, Aryas as well as non-Aryas. *Pur* represented a settlement which is invariably enclosed by a wall made of stone, red-bricks, mud-bricks or mud, all of which have been encountered in the Harappan excavations. The other term *vṛtra* (from √vṛ, 'to cover', 'to enclose'), also signified a walled settlement, but the plural *vṛtrāṇi* refers to the inhabitance of such settlements. The stories relating to destruction of *vṛtra* fall into two categories. In most instances, *vṛtra* represents a demon that obstructed the flow of rivers and prevented the clouds from releasing rain. But, in several instances, the episodes relate to actual fights for the capture of walled settlements. Occasionally, the interior of these walled settlements, with passages or pathways criss-crossing the built-up area, was comparable to a spider's web (*aurṇavābham*). This is fairly well-suggested by the Harappan archaeological records from the early urban phase.

The two other terms *durga* and *vṛjana* also represent fortified settlements. The term *durga* means 'difficult to access', and *vṛjana* (from √*vṛ*, 'to cover' +*jana*, 'people') an enclosure for people or a settlement. In one case, the term *durga* appears as an adjective of the term *pur*, suggesting thereby a 'settlement difficult to access' (*puraḥ durgaḥ*, 1.41.3). In another case, the term appears in association with a word for 'house', both in the locative case, *duroṇe durge* or a 'house or settlement difficult to access', and refers to Indra destroying thousands of enemies hidden inside these strongholds (4.28.3). Plans were hatched (*kratva*, 4.28.3) to access the stronghold (*durga*), fights undertaken to capture the invincible citadels (*azre durge*, 8.27.18), prayers chanted for deflecting the flaming missiles (*aśani*, 8.27.18) hurled from inside these citadels and defeated inmates put into captivity. As for *vṛjana*, the poets express the desire to capture enclosures belonging to the enemies and lodge themselves inside them (1.51.15, 1.128.7).

The Commercial Context

The 10,000-odd stanzas of the *Ṛgveda* bear eloquent testimony to a flourishing long-distance trade, both overseas and overland. There are copious references to people venturing out on the high seas in quest of wealth and fame. Consider the terms *bhujyu* (*bhujyuṃ arṇ asaḥ samudrāt*, 1.117.14), *saniṣyavaḥ* (*saniṣyavaḥ saṃcaraṇe samudre na*, 1.56.2) and *śravasyavaḥ* (*śravasyavaḥ samudre na*, 1.48.3), all of which figure in stanzas relating to seafaring. Bhujyu, the name of a chief, indicates a person venturing out in quest of wealth. The term is derived from *bhuj*, meaning 'resources', and *yu*, a typical old Vedic verb meaning 'to reach out', 'to go after'. The episode of Bhujyu figures prominently in several stanzas of the text. Bhujyu together with his father and other associates were sailing in several ships when suddenly his ship started sinking on account of maritime disturbances. Bhujyu was, however, rescued by the Aśvins, who were master navigators and kept sailing most of the time. Similarly, the term *sanisyavaḥ* also means people venturing out in the quest of wealth (*sanis*, 'wealth', + *yu*, 'to go after'). Likewise, the term *śravasyavaḥ* means people venturing out in quest of fame (*śravas*, fame + *yu*, 'to go after'). Allusions to piracy are also not wanting in the text. In the event of the loss of direction, the flight path of seafaring birds proved helpful.

As for overland trade, poets refer to armed groups of robbers who intercepted the caravans at difficult points of the journey and bargained for as much of the goods they could appropriate from the traders. Armed escorts did not always succeed in containing these wayside marauders. The dangers of wayfaring, commercial or otherwise, were common to all societies in all ages. However, this may have increased with the decay of urban places and the regression of state authority.

Trading activities were organized mostly on a private basis by groups of individuals with or without marginal support from chiefs along the way. The incidence of metallic money was limited, the bulk of trade being carried on through barter. Terms for sale, purchase and lease were known just as for customs duty. The term *śulka* appears twice in the text, once in the sense of a wager, and another time in the sense of toll or tax. The sale of substandard and underweight goods was common but there was no way to address the malaise. Loans were taken and repaid along with interest, but failure to repay led to enslavement of the debtor by the creditor. The exchanges took place through peddlers moving in small or large groups. Frequently, the bardic composers themselves acted as the medium of commodity exchange between far-off places. On other occasions, they were a part of long-distance caravans. The term *vaṇik*, meaning a trader, occurs twice in the *Ṛgveda*, once referring to a bardic caravaneer (*vaṇije dīghaśravase*, 1.112.11), and another time to a crafty trader (*vaṇik, vanku*, 5.45.6). Some idea of the commodities exchanged is also provided by the goods collected by *Ṛgvedic* bards from their patrons. These included horses, camels, donkeys, cattle, goats and sheep, chariots, objects of gold and brass as well as solid blocks of these metals, textiles of different types, precious gems, metallic money, slaves, brights with glittering jewellery and items of food. A part of this was consumed by the recipients, but the rest was disposed of through barter or money transactions, besides presentation to prospective patrons, chiefs, queens and others. All this gives us some idea of how things were shaping on the commercial front during the third millennium BC.

An examination of the term 'paṇi', which occurs nearly fifty times in the *Ṛgveda* and has been the focus of divergent comments and interpretations, seems imperative here. There is no doubt that the Paṇis were affluent people and that their affluence depended on trade, stock raising and banking activities. In the absence of any public banking system, the Paṇis probably functioned as bankers and financers of the third millennium BC, whose co-operation was basic to all commercial activity. The banking dimension of the Paṇis' activities is well-suggested by the expression *ahadṛśaḥ paṇim* or the Paṇi who keeps a record of the past days. A regular term for the usurer or banker is *grathin*, which also has the same meaning as *ahadṛśaḥ* (8.66.10). This is peculiar to the usurer or the banker whose profits multiply with the number of days that pass. Another passage has the expression *paṇinām bṛbu mūrdhanya stha* (6.45.31), meaning the chief of the Paṇis takes a high position among his people. The position is said to be as high as the banks of the Gangā (*urukakṣo na gāngyaḥ*). The term *Bṛbu* does not signify a carpenter, as suggested by certain scholars. The carpenter surely had considerable importance as the maker and mender of boats, carts, household furniture, doors, windows and so forth. But he could not have been a money-spinner either for himself or the community. This is a role that fits quite well with the activities of a banker or moneychanger in the commercial milieu of the third millennium BC.

The wealth accumulated by the banker not only enriched the Paṇis but also gave rise to greed and jealousy in the minds of other people. This is fairly well-suggested by the fact that most of the bardic references to the Paṇis are of a critical nature. The bards constantly prey on their wealth and it is sometimes stolen. But there is no mention of an actual fight to forcibly take away this wealth. Such restraint seems to have been less because of the armed guards of the Paṇis and more because of the Paṇis' crucial role in the promotion of trade, which was appreciated by bards as well as chiefs. This is why there is no evidence of a single encounter with the Paṇis. In certain cases, bards even co-operated with the Paṇis in order to augment the latter's resources, as seen in a passage of the Sixth Book (6.45.33) which states that as soon as the Angirāses completed their prayers to the gods, the chief of the Paṇis (*paṇeḥ naraḥ*, 6.45.31–3) was showered with fabulous wealth. We need only add here that many of the passages on the Paṇis were done by the Angira bards and that the Angirāses were the earliest proponents of the bardic ideology. The importance of the Paṇis to the bards who speak about them is also well-suggested by the fact that in some of these passages the term 'paṇi' is the equivalent of wealth and is strongly desired by the concerned bards as in *paṇim imahe* (8.45.14).

The Age of Decay

As for the ruined settlements, littered with burials, there is a single expression (*armake vailasthāne*, 1.133.3), which occurs twice in the same passage of the First Book. In both these instances, the words are used in the locative case with the first part serving as the adjective. Taken together, the expression means 'in the ugly or awesome place of the dead'. However, the term *armaka* does not have a satisfactory derivation in the Vedic dialect. Probably, it was the Vedic synonym of a Dravidian vocable *ara-mana* or *armana*, meaning 'house of the king or a "palace"', used here in a derogatory sense. In the Harappan context, many of the decaying settlements were erstwhile centres of political power and could accordingly be described as 'palaces'. But, the fortifications which enclosed these 'palaces' also contained several sprawling graveyards as at Harappa. These burial grounds appear to be well-represented by the term *vailasthāna* or *mahavailasthāna*. From the word *vila* or *bila*, which is a regular term for a pit or hole, *vailasthāna* would mean cracked, split, to be separated. From *vil* in Tamil, *vailasthāna* may also mean the place where the dead are finally separated from their relatives, a burial ground. This is precisely what the city of Harappa must have looked like within fifty or hundred years of its abandonment. Interestingly, the term *vailasthāna* anticipates the much later place-name 'Mohenjo-daro', or 'the Mound of the Dead', given to it by brick robbers who encountered massive graveyards and numerous unburied skeletons at the site. .

Synchronizing these events, one may suggest that the strife for the capture of the walled resource centres called *pur, durga, vṛtra* and *vṛjana* marked the onset of urban decline and commercial regression, which destabilized the economy and created conditions for social upheaval. At this earliest phase, the calamities, natural or man-made, were marginal in effect and confined to specific regions. Another fifty or hundred years later, the devastations of different types compounded and engulfed the entire Greater Indus Valley with people dying from famines, scarcity, epidemics, inundations, earthquakes, disruption of communications and raging armed conflicts for subsistence and survival. About this time, many of the settlements, like Mohenjo-daro and Harappa may have been littered with unburied corpses, with no civic administration to take care of the dead or the living. The terms *armaka* and *vailasthāna* appear to justify a situation like this. Even the passage in which these two expressions occur refers to large-scale killing of the inhabitants of these places by armed groups of attackers. The clusters of unburied skeletons, which fired the imagination of certain archaeologists who thought a massacre took place at Mohenjo-daro,[12] may have been people dying in large numbers from natural calamities, like famines, epidemics, earthquakes as well as from attacks by wandering armed people looking for new habitations and resources.

Whether it was the capture of a stronghold or a ruined place, the attackers and attacked are invariably distinguished on the basis of a religious ideology rather than on the basis of skin colour or physical features, suggesting thereby that both the groups were compatriots, one of which identified itself as the worshippers of divinities (*Daivya Hotāraḥ*) and denounced the other as non-believers (*Devānām Dviṣaḥ*, 1.133.7). Other terms used for the non-believers are *Adeva* ('without Gods', 5.61.6), *Amanta* ('mindless', 10.22.8), *Atrātar* ('non-protecting'), *Arādhas* ('non-giving'), *Ayajnyan* ('devoid of sacrifices', 7.6.3), *Aśraddhān* ('disrespectful', 7.6.3), *Amitra* ('unfriendly', 1.133.1),

Anyavratah̩ ('practising other rituals', 10.22.8), *Akarma* ('non-sacrificing', 10.22.8), *Amānuṣāḥ* ('inferior mortals', 10.22.8) and *Mṛdhravācaḥ* ('ill-spoken', 7.6.3). The enemies looked hefty (*Ambhṛnam*, 1.133.5) with reddish spikes in their hands (*Piśangbhṛṣṭim*, 1.133.5), were disrespectful of Indra (*Anindra*, 1.133.1), wicked (*Piśāchim*, 1.133.5) and the practitioners of witchcraft (*Yātumatinām*, 1.133.2–3).

Consider how the walled settlements must have looked a couple of centuries later. As many of these places were completely deserted, the structures became worn out and dilapidated in many parts to justify the bardic expression 'dwellings of ancient times' (*pratnasya okasa*) and the locative 'in the dwellings of ancient times' (*pratneṣu dhāmaṣu*). Some of these ancient Harappan settlements may have been still partly habitable, which encouraged wandering groups of bardic composers and their followers to settle down at these places. The term 'ancient settlements' appears frequently in the compositions of bards, who may have lived a few centuries after the decay of the Harappan settlements set in. In one case, it is stated that the God Rudra shone in all those ancient settlements (*pratneṣu dhāmaṣu*, 8.13.20), where the bards prayed in his honour. Another passage of the eighth *Maṇḍala* refers to *Priyamedha-Angirāsas* lodging themselves in settlements belonging to antiquity (8.69.18).

The antiquity of the Priyamedhas, who are listed after Dadhici and Angira, and before Kaṇva, Atri and Manu (1.139.9) seems to match fairly well with the antiquity of the deserted Harappan settlements in Sindh, Punjab and Rajasthan. That the Priyamedhas belong to this area can be witnessed from their reference to the land of seven rivers, which flowed into the sea (8.69.12), a phenomenon, which would not be relevant to either Afghanistan or eastern Iran. Such descriptions may have continued until the deserted and untended Harappan structures slowly turned into large mounds. Such mound formation would have taken between three to five centuries from when depopulation of the Harappan centres started. For more accurate reflections, one must however turn to knowledgeable archaeologists.

Significance of the Viṣṭāśpa-Kakṣivān Episode

Considering that the *Ṛgveda* and the *Avesta* were sister documents focusing on the activities of the earliest Vedic speakers and earliest Avestan speakers of the Indo-Iranian subcontinent during the Middle and Late Bronze Ages, certain episodes connecting the two ideologies are discussed here. This is all the more important since after long years of pioneering research in the field of Avestan studies, it has not been possible for scholars to provide a firm historical date for either Zarathuṣṭra or Viṣṭāśpa. As for Viṣṭāśpa, a close associate and powerful supporter of Zarathuṣṭra, the name occurs in three different contexts. In ascending order, Viṣṭāśpa figures as the father of Darius-I in one of his inscriptions. The next reference to Viṣṭāśpa is in the Avestan texts. The third reference to Viṣṭāśpa appears in a passage of the first *Maṇḍala* of the *Ṛgveda*.

There is no problem with the first context. But the Avestan texts, which are stratified on the basis of phonological principals, are assigned to the second half of the second millennium BC. However, in the absence of any firm correlation with known historical events, the chronology would appear to be more presumptuous than factual and there may have been several persons of this name at different periods. The third reference to Viṣṭāśpa relates to the poet-son of a merchant father and it occurs in a trade-specific context, which may help us to determine the approximate date of Viṣṭāśpa and the *Ṛgvedic* poet angered by him.

The poet-son composed invocations to gods on behalf of different chiefs and collected fabulous gifts from them. The merchant father on the other hand earned profits by selling or exchanging parts of these goods, which were in excess of the family's requirements. The family appears to have been tormented by the chief Viṣṭāśpa and forced to migrate from Iran to the province of Sindh. Considering that the chiefdom of Viṣṭāśpa was in the south-eastern part of Iran, a direct trek along the Makran Coast would land a person in the coastal regions of the lower Indus plain.

Kakṣivān (1.122.9, 13–15), who makes an angry reference to Iṣṭāśva or Viṣṭāśpa and left the country in the company of his merchant father to reach the Lower Indus Basin, composed several *Dānastuti* passages there in honour of the local chief Bhavya Svanaya, who was said to be ruling on the banks of the Indus (*sindhau adhi kṣiyanti*). The chief, in his turn, offered the priest prestigious goods like chariots, Sindhian red horses, gold coins, cattle, slaves and servants, besides maidens in fabulous bridal costumes. Interestingly, the poet-son delivered all these goods to his merchant father as soon as he received them. This reconstruction, which has been treated at length elsewhere, is intended to focus on a time when marginal commodity exchanges were still continuing on the Indo-Iranian subcontinent. Such a process did not really depend on large urban places, all of which had disappeared by the close of the third millennium BC. Accordingly, the compositions may well date back to the first quarter of the second millennium BC. The link-up with Viṣṭāśpa may, however, place the compositions of Kakṣivān during the first half of the eighteenth century BC.

Unlike Viṣṭāśpa, who appears in at least one historical document, Zarathuṣṭra, the founder of the Ahuric faith, remains confined to the Avestan texts. Some scholars would like to see him as a contemporary of the Buddha and accordingly place him in the sixth century BC. Judging on the basis of tenuous evidence from certain Assyrian inscriptions, other scholars would like to place him towards the beginning of the eleventh century BC. Since no historical dates for Zarathuṣṭra are forthcoming, we may turn to the Zarathuṣṭrian religious tradition in this connection.

According to tradition, Zarathuṣṭra was born on 6th of Farvardin 30 of the Zarathuṣṭrian Religious Era (26 March 1767 BC). After much struggle in his native land on the banks of the Oxus, Zarathuṣṭra arrived at the court of Viṣṭāśpa, the warrior-poet chief of the Helmand Valley. The atmosphere of rivalry at the court of Viṣṭāśpa and his indifference may have angered poet Kakṣivān, who cursed the chief and sought safer haven, sometime during the middle of the eighteenth century BC. One may add here that Zarathuṣṭra was the son of Soma oblator, Pourūṣāspa, who himself was preceded by four generations or lineages represented by Kereshaspa, Aithya, Trita and Vivangvān, each one mentioned together with his successor, and furnishing a total of nine Soma-related characters. Reckoning that each generation was about twenty-five to thirty years, the earliest of the Soma oblators of Iran would go back to the middle of the twentieth century BC.

Zarathuṣṭra's father, Pourūṣāspa of the Spitama clan of an Iranian tribe, raised cattle and was famous for his horses. His mother, Dughdav, was known for her enlightened ideas. The family lived near the bank of the Oxus River in present-day Central Asia. Zarathuṣṭra, inquisitive by nature, was a consummate thinker. For over ten years, he and his small fellowship of companions were harassed and tortured. With determination and innate wisdom and a grave risk to his life, he decided to bring his divine doctrine to the chief ruler, Viṣṭāśpa. Some of these rulers were both warriors and intellectuals and were called *kavis*, or sages. Kavi Viṣṭāśpa of the Helmand Valley, towards the south-east, was a powerful person and like other *kavis*, a man of learning. Zarathuṣṭra's enemies had already reached the court of Viṣṭāśpa to doom his mission. Zarathuṣṭra, undaunted, faced the King and his court but it was a struggle of epic proportions. It took two years of perseverance to deliberate and deliver the divine message to the king and queen, their court and people; to eradicate all evil ideas, intoxicating rituals, bloody sacrifices, and duping dozes, and to replace them with 'Good Thoughts' (*Humaita*), 'Good Words' (*Hukaita*), and 'Good Deeds' (*Hukairya*). Zarathuṣṭra was forty-two years old at that time. King Viṣṭāśpa, Queen Hutaosa, their children, and the people underwent a complete transformation. The princes forsook the throne and became zealous missionaries. The result was that the Good Religion spread far and wide within the lifetime of Zarathuṣṭra. Satisfied that his 'best wishes [had] come true', Zarathuṣṭra passed away peacefully at the ripe age of seventy-seven years and forty days.

This account of Zarathuṣṭra's life might place the beginnings of Soma oblations started by Vivasvān, a Soma priest who was later raised to the position of a divinity, sometime about the middle of the twentieth century BC. Considering also that the Soma oblations were a later adjunct of *Daiva* worship, the beginning of *Daiva* worship itself may go back a century or two earlier, possibly about the close of the third millennium BC.

If the aforementioned account of Zarathuṣṭra and Viṣṭāśpa is any indication, the new faith originated in a land dominated by the Sagis or Saka Iranians who gave their name to the country Sagistan or Seistan. The Sagis, who may have been deeply influenced by the Gathic dialect, divinities and rituals as early as the eighteenth century BC itself could be potential disseminators of these influences throughout the Eurasian region in the wake of their migration towards the north west and elsewhere beyond the frontiers of Iran.

The wide acceptability that a monotheistic system found first on the eastern and the north-eastern tracts of Iran and later on the western Iranian tracts may or may not have been prompted by some characteristic ethnic trades manifesting themselves through the Magi priests of Mazdian sects. Though paleo-ethnological beliefs and ideas are inaccessible at the moment, the devolution of ancient religious ideas could not have been altogether unrelated to divergent ethnic beliefs and practices.

Given the present state of our knowledge, an attempt to situate the beginnings of *Daiva* ideology and the Ahuric doctrine in their historical context cannot be definitive. There is, however, no denying the fact that ideologies and belief systems are the products of their social environment. From this angle, the exercise becomes more worthwhile than the existing ideas that seek to situate the two systems and their concerned dialects in the social vacuum of the mid-second millennium BC and an imaginary central homeland in south Turkmenistan, all based on a hypothetical linguistic idea. As we have already stated, the Indo-Iranian subcontinent had turned into a cultural wilderness after the eighteenth century BC. As for the central homeland in south Turkmenistan, there is no evidence of ethno-cultural dispersal in the archaeological sense of the term. Moreover, archaeology is neither a grammar nor a lexicon so as to tell us what the people spoke, in which dialects and in which areas.

The Funerary Horizon

The regressive character of cremation-related practices outside the Indo-Iranian borderlands needs explaining. In Iran and neighbouring Afghanistan, the practice of cremation may have been discouraged by the preachings of Mazdian against polluting the fire, the water and the earth. However, the preachings of Mazdian against the practice of burial did not find favour with the ethnic Iranians, who refused to give up their traditional mode of disposal of the dead, so much so that the Achaemenian emperors, who were great devotees of Ahur Mazda, preferred majestic tombs as their resting places. Second, the period of Indo-Iranian dispersal towards the north-west and south-east coincided with a period of hyper-arid episodes, which caused widespread desiccation and a corresponding depletion of the green cover. The small groups of refugees, who left their decaying urban and proto-urban settlements to establish new homes in the marginal oases along some of the river valleys could ill-afford to further reduce the tree cover for full or partial cremations, even as a token of elite presence. Third, in the Harappan area itself, full or partial cremations were just one of the several modes of disposal of the dead and much less widespread than burials. The practice probably signified an ethno-religious community, which formed part of the power elite in certain areas where it has been observed. Since the basic idea was the sanctification of the departed soul, cremation may have been projected as a marker of the power elite and may explain the extremely occasional nature of cremation-related practices in south-eastern Europe and northern Central Asia during the early second millennium BC. In the Mariupol cemetery, situated on the Sea of Azov, opposite the town of Mariupol, only one (no. 21) out of a total of 124 graves shows the signs of cremation. In the Maikop region also, the signs of cremation come only from the royal graves.[13]

Similarly, the Andronovo people, who inhabited a vast area from middle Yenisey to western Kazakhstan, did not always follow the same funerary customs. For example, the cemeteries that have been investigated on the Yenisey and the Ob Rivers, indicate that some of the dead have been buried, while others have been cremated with the actual remains (of the cremated person) preserved in stone chests.[14] The Andronovo people, who are said to have entered Kirghizia and the Ferghana Valley from the north and settled at different places, practised diverse funerary rituals suggestive of sub-ethnic communities within the Andronovo culture. For instance, the Tautara cemetery on the northern slopes of the Karatan chain shows the northern tradition of carrying out burials in cemeteries situated apart in stone enclosures or under barrows formed by bringing in earth or a mixture of earth and stone. Excavations at the Murghab settlement of Tahirbay-3, however, have brought to light evidence of partial cremation alongside the internments.[15] During the Neolithic Age, the people of the Kazakh Steppes practised burials, particularly sitting burials, often under the floor of a room. Certain Neolithic groups, however, who may have constituted sub-ethnic communities in the vast Kazakh Steppes, practised post-cremation burials. The most interesting grave of this type was found at the village of Zhelezinka, 100 km. from the Pen'ki site. Here, burial was preceded by cremation. The grave goods included a sickle-shaped headdress fashioned out of bone, a necklace consisting of animal teeth and large shell beads, besides the phalanges of a Kulan or a wild ass, stained with red ochre.[16]

In terms of diffusion of the funerary practices, the only possibility would be from north-western South Asia to Central Asia and south-eastern Europe, although the delimiting factor would have been the absence of full or partial cremation in the entire intermediate zone of Iran and Afghanistan during the third or second millennium BC. The evidence of cremation, the use of red ochre and the depiction of the sun motif on funeral pottery, which frequently characterized burials of Kurgan people in the north Pontic region during late third and early second millennium BC, are said to be typical elements of the religion of the Indo-European-speaking peoples and specifically of the eastern ones in which, the fire and the Sun cults are most developed.[17] The cultural equipment of royal graves at Maikop and Tsarskaia, also associated with the Kurgan people, show close links with Hissar II and III in northern Iran.[18] Some of the Harappan elements, which struck roots in the adjoining areas of northern Iran and south Turkmenistan undergoing a cultural synthesis, were evidently part of the enterprising families, who, following the destabilization of the world system during late third millennium BC, may have moved out in different directions, the wealthier and more powerful towards Syria, Turkey and south-eastern Europe and the less well-to-do towards the lower Murghab delta, southern Tajikistan and the Kazakh Steppes.

The feuding groups of scholars, who for quite different reasons describe cremation as the chief characteristic of the Aryan lifestyle, may thus find it difficult to wish away the funerary data embedded in the *Ṛgveda* or the correspondence of this information with the available archaeological record in the Greater Indus Valley during the third millennium BC. For those scholars, who vigorously argue that the Aryans migrated to South Asia during the mid-second millennium BC, it would be imperative to explain why the chief marker of a people belonging to the mid-second millennium BC is encountered in north-western South Asia about a millennium earlier (2500–1900 BC). Scholars who think that cremation is an ethno-religious marker, which distinguished the ancient Hindus [*sic*] and their successors from rival ethno-religious communities, may not find the practice of burials or post-exposure burials, so vividly described in the *Ṛgveda* to be wholesome stuff.

These observations indicate the possibility of cultural shifts from northern Iran and the adjoining south Turkmenistan towards south-eastern Europe during the late third and early second millennium BC. During the course of hyperactive continental trade between the Greater Indus Valley and Mesopotamia, some of the Harappan elements and Harappan influences may have struck roots in certain Turkmenistan sites like Altyn-depe. Following the decline of proto-urban settlements in Iran and south Central Asia about 2300 BC, these Harappan influences may have moved together with the Iranians into south-eastern Europe and north Central Asia, particularly, the Kazakh Steppes.

A survey of funerary behaviour in Asia and Europe during the third and second millennium BC would at once show that the earliest evidence of cremations belongs to north-western South Asia during the third millennium BC. Outside this region, the evidence of full or partial cremation is not only extremely occasional but also invariably belongs to the second millennium BC. However, judging by the rarity of cremation contexts in both the areas, the Harappan influence relating to cremations appears to have been a regressive phenomenon. Even in the Harappan area, cremation was just one of the several funerary practices, probably confined to particular ethno-religious groups.

A comparative survey of archaeological contexts in Iran, Afghanistan and south Central Asia between the fourth and second millennium BC suggests a south to north movement of peoples and cultures.[19] The earliest of these relate to movements from central Iranian tracts, first during the mid-fourth millennium BC and then again during the late fourth millennium BC, influencing the Chalcolithic cultures in the oasis settlements in the foothills of the northern Kopet Dag Mountains.[20] The settled communities of south Turkmenistan achieved a particularly significant level of development during the late fourth to the early third millennium BC in the wake of widespread interactions involving north-western South Asia, Mesopotamia, Iran and south Central Asia. At that time, they found themselves included in a system of increasingly close cultural ties and ethnic shifts, which encompassed an extensive area in Iran, Afghanistan and north-western Indo-Pak regions.[21]

During the early and mid-third millennium BC, the high tide of continental comers between Mesopotamia and the Indus Valley through Afghanistan, Iran and south Central Asia witnessed great cultural interactions, which may have followed the small but powerful presence of Harappans and Mesopotamians in this intermediate region. The characteristic Harappan influences are already noticeable at the Early Bronze Age settlement of Altyn-depe in the form of the Swastika symbol, Harappan writing, divination sticks and dices made of ivory, and the use of the Harappan cubit system in constructing buildings.[22]

Notes

1. M. Witzel, 'On the Localisation of Vedic Texts and Schools (Materials on Vedic Sakhas, 7)', in *India and the Ancient World: History, Trade and Culture Before AD 650*, ed. G. Pollet, P.H.L. Eggermont Jubilee Volume, Leuven: Departement Oriëntalistiek, 1987, pp. 173–213; Witzel, 'Tracing the Vedic Dialects', in *Dialectes dans les litte'ratures indo-aryennes*, ed. Colette Caillat, Paris: Institut de Civilisation Indienne, 1989, pp. 97–264; Witzel, 'Early Indian History: Linguistic and Textual Parameters', in *The Indo-Aryans of Ancient South Asia*, ed. G. Erdosy, Indian Philology and South Asian Studies 1, Berlin and New York: de Gruyter, 1995, pp. 85–125; Witzel, 'Rigvedic History: Poets, Chieftains and Polities', in *The Indo-Aryans of Ancient South Asia*, ed. Erdosy, pp. 307–52; Witzel, 'Substrate Languages in Old Indo-Aryan', *Electronic Journal of Vedic Studies*, vol. 5, no. 1, September 1999, p. 96.
2. K. Hoffmann, 'Avestan Language', in *Encyclopaedia Iranica*, ed. Y. Ehsan, vol. III, London and New York: Routledge and Kegan Paul, 1989, pp. 47–62.
3. M. Boyce, 'Avestan People', in *Encyclopaedia Iranica*, ed. Ehsan, vol. III, pp. 62–6.
4. A. Ghosh, ed., *An Encyclopaedia of Indian Archaeology*, vol. 1, Indian Council of Historical Research, New Delhi: Munshiram Manoharlal, 1989, pp. 81, 316.
5. M. Dhavalikar and S. Atre, 'The Fire Cult and Virgin Sacrifice: Some Harappan Rituals', in *Old Problems and New Perspectives in the Archaeology of South Asia*, ed. J.M. Kenoyer, Wisconsin

Archaeology Reports, vol. 2, Department of Anthropology, Madison: Wisconsin University Press, 1989, pt. 4, chapter 20, pp. 193–207.

6. Ibid.
7. A. Parpola, *Deciphering the Indus Script*, 1994; repr., Cambridge: Cambridge University Press, 1997.
8. V.M. Masson, 'The Bronze Age in Khorasan and Transoxania', in *History of Civilizations of Central Asia*, ed. A.H. Dani and V.M. Masson, vol. 1, Paris: UNESCO, 1992; repr., 1st Indian edn., Delhi: Motilal Banarsidass, 1999.
9. Ibid.
10. M. Gimbutas, 'The Neolithic, Chalcolithic and Copper Ages in the North Pontic Area', in *The Prehistory of Eastern Europe, Mesolithic, Neolithic and Copper Age Cultures in Russia and the Baltic Area*, pt. I, American School of Prehistory Research, Peabody Museum, Harvard University, Bulletin No. 20, Cambridge, Massachusetts: Peabody Museum, 1956.
11. R.N. Nandi, *Ideology and Environment: Situating the Origin of Vedic Culture*, Delhi: Akaar, 2009, chapters 4–7.
12. R.E.M. Wheeler, 'Harappa 1946: The Defences and Cemetery R 37', in *The Indus Civilization*, Cambridge: Cambridge University Press, 1953.
13. Gimbutas, 'Neolithic, Chalcolithic and Copper Ages'.
14. Masson, 'The Bronze Age in Khorasan and Transoxania'.
15. Ibid.
16. A.P. Derevyanko and D. Dorj, 'Neolithic Tribes in Northern Parts of Central Asia', in *History of Civilizations of Central Asia*, ed. A.H. Dani and V.M. Masson, vol. 1, Paris: UNESCO, 1992; repr., 1st Indian edn., Delhi: Motilal Banarsidass, 1999, p. 185.
17. Gimbutas, 'Neolithic, Chalcolithic and Copper Ages'.
18. Ibid.

19. A.H. Dani and B.K. Thapar, 'The Indus Civilization', in *History of Civilizations of Central Asia*, ed. A.H. Dani and V.M. Masson, vol. 1, Paris: UNESCO, 1992; repr., 1st Indian edn., Delhi: Motilal Banarsidass, 1999, pp. 301–2.
20. Masson, 'The Bronze Age in Khorasan and Transoxania'.
21. Ibid.
22. Ibid.

3

Language and Social Change

THE PRESENT CHAPTER seeks to understand the social processes in north-western South Asia during the Middle Bronze Age and begins by posing few relevant questions that have either been conveniently ignored or inadequately answered. The Middle Bronze Age was a transition period not so much from the Early to the Late Bronze Age as of a social system undergoing radical changes through synergy and internal dynamics under the heat of persistent social and geo-climatic devastations. On the outer fringe of this period was a flourishing urban civilization which entered a longish phase of decay and disintegration towards the close of the third millennium BC. On the inner side of this time frame was a civilization characterized by decadent urban places, dwindling craft and commerce and an overarching religious ideology. For an understanding of the former, one has to depend on archaeological evidence. The latter scenario, however, is better understood on the basis of a large oral text, supplemented by evidence and insights from archaeology. Contrary to this perception, which finds support in certain processualist writings,[1] the general tendency has been to describe the situation in terms of two unrelated social systems separated by a wide margin of time, one indigenous and the other immigrant, one urban and the other pastoral. Such fixed ideas are as much a victim of 'path dependency' as those invoked by certain scholars[2] to criticize the hypothesis that Harappan inscriptions represent a definite language.

The question of an urban-pastoral divide is irrelevant in the Harappan context that shows the simultaneous existence of pastoral, agricultural and commercially-integrated urban societies, all interactive and interdependent. The post-urban scenario may be devoid of megacities, but there is no dearth of marginal urban communities coexisting with agricultural, agro-pastoral and pastoral communities besides coastal fishing colonies and the colonies of miners and gem-cutters on the highlands. The question of migration, whether from outside South Asia or from inside it, is inconsequential. Migration from Europe, if at all, preceded the Middle Bronze Age by a few thousand years and has nothing to do with historical developments being underlined here. We may, however, draw attention to the fact that extreme episodes of cold-dry phase during the Early Holocene (8000–5000 BC) phase in Europe and a wet-and-warm regimen in much of Asia and Africa may have driven native Europeans (not Indo-Europeans) towards more hospitable southern latitudes. This diaspora may have participated in the creation of a loose Eurasian dialect family, which branched off subsequently for reasons of political adventurism, economic enterprise, missionary activities, besides adverse geo-climatic conditions. Though the priorities on the wish-list of certain scholars are hard to sideline, the least one can try is to address certain basic issues which may help to place the whole problem in perspective.

First, the oral text which consists of 10,000-odd religious songs does not give any evidence of migration from outside South Asia or the memories of any such land. Second, it has been ignored, perhaps conveniently, that the most widely invoked divinity in the text claims that the land of the seven rivers was his domain. The claims of divinities are indeed the sentiments of the composers themselves. Third, there is no dispute about the fact that the hymns of the *Ṛgveda* were composed in north-western South Asia, which is precisely the area occupied by the Harappan people. Fourth, even by conservative estimates, the earliest hymns of the text can be dated to about the beginning of the second millennium BC—between 1900 and 1700 BC to be precise—while the latest compositions can be assigned to 1200 BC.[3] Fifth, latest studies of Harappan chronology show that the Late Harappan period, which began towards the end of the third millennium BC, continued with marginal urban places as late as 1500 BC and even afterwards.[4]

This means that the Vedic-speaking communities, whoever they may have been, were contemporaries of the Harappans for at least half a millennium and as compatriots experienced the same historical processes during this period. Finally, the hymns of the *Ṛgveda* represent a religious ideology that lays great emphasis on divination of forces of nature, both good and bad, outlining a specific prayer liturgy and an articulated dialect to practise it. Though the signification of a religious ideology has been recognized by some scholars,[5] there has not been any attempt to contextualize it historically. An ideology—political, economic, religious—does not originate in social emptiness. Rather, there have to be overriding compulsions in both nature and society to motivate such a process. Why the text lays so much emphasis on pleasing or placating icons in nature and society, on good moral behaviour and pursuit of cosmic laws, and on catastrophic events, constant fear of death from disease and civil war, besides natural calamities, has never been asked. It also remains to be explained why out of a score of terms signifying house, residence or settlement, so much importance is attached to strongholds identified as *pur*, *durga* and *vṛjana* and also why the Vedic speakers were trying to capture these strongholds and lodge themselves inside them.

It is the innate logic of historical dialectics that every society unless in absolute isolation undergoes changes, slow or fast, depending on the internal dynamic of the social components or interaction with the outer world, both human and natural. It has been demonstrated that this area witnessed transformation right from the beginning of pre-historic period. The Harappan civilization itself has been stratified on the basis of these changes, processual and artifactual, the latter reflecting on the former. Things could not have been different during the Middle Bronze Age which began with the gradual disintegration of an urban civilization, both intra-regional and inter-regional.

The idea that the Harappan inscriptions represent a sign system without any linguistic value[6] would suggest that this system was universally understood in a broad spectrum, multilingual space. This means that writing could exist without words so long as it fulfilled specified requirements of the society, political, economic and religious. This does not, however, mean that the Harappan region was devoid of the spoken word. Rather several linguistic specimens coexisted in this area from very early times as a means of communication through the spoken word only. There is no archaeological corroboration of such linguistic diversity but the hymns of the *Ṛgveda*, which almost synchronized with the Harappan urbanization, refer to the unproductive dialect or dialects that were unfit for saying prayers. Some of the ethnic groups that used these dialects were the Pakthas (Pakhtoons of today), Bhalanas (people of the Bolan Pass or Bolan Valley) and Śivas (Siboi of the Greeks or people living around Sibi in the Sindh province of Pakistan). Besides, there were variants of the Vedic dialect itself, sometimes described as corrupt or unintelligible.

Moreover, a society as complex as the Harappan would have had oral texts of varied size and importance. But these have not survived, in the absence of any articulate system of preservation and transmission. A form of writing to maintain administrative and economic records cannot also be ruled out. Perhaps such records cannot be effective, let alone survive in the absence of scripted documents. By contrast, religious texts can and have actually survived through the centuries by means of a compact system of rote. As such, a liturgical dialect can preserve valuable information on social, political, economic processes like in the case of the existing *Śākalya* text. A new liturgy can bring into existence new dialects, processed from the older spoken dialects. This seems to have happened all over the world like in the case of Hieratic of the ancient Egyptian religion, liturgical Hebrew of Judaism, liturgical Arabic of Islam during the seventh century in Arabia and the Mantra dialect of the Old Vedic religion of South Asia. Priestly interests also prevent a dialect from altogether disappearing like in the case of Hebrew which continued as a priestly dialect even after the disappearance of its spoken forms; the latter once again got revived in recent times.

With the disappearance of the Harappan sign system in the wake of widespread decay and disintegration of an urban civilization from the beginning of the second millennium BC, the importance of the spoken word and the need to preserve and transmit through it certain essential forms of knowledge like magic, medicine and religion must have been felt increasingly. The relevance of an oral religious literature which represented an ideology of nature worship and served as the vehicle of this ideology seems to have become imperative about this time. The ideology tried to please or placate the various forces of nature and induce them to protect worshippers against catastrophic events in nature and society and grant them whatever was needed for a happy and prosperous existence. Since the purpose was special, the words also had to be likewise and different from mundane speech. This might explain the beginning of a Mantra dialect of the *Ṛgveda* which emerged from a vernacular form of the Vedic dialect, the latter preceding the former by several centuries.

The vernacular Vedic dialect stood halfway between the Mantra dialect and various spoken dialects like Prākṛt, Dravidian and Munda. The vernacular Vedic which was confined to conversation among the members of priestly families accumulated substantial substrate influences from these spoken dialects in the course of interactions and communication between the members of the priestly families and the society at large. Since all the relatives were not immediately concerned with the liturgy, their familiarity with the Mantra dialect was not even peripheral. Given their concerns with the larger society, however, they were fairly conversant with the spoken dialects.

Many of these lesser members of these families may have grown up with one or the other of the spoken dialects as their first language.

As the Mantra dialect and the accompanying liturgy grew in importance and covered new territory, the craft became a lucrative enterprise. It may have motivated some of these half-learners to try their hand at the Mantra compositions and carve out a fortune in the political circles. Perhaps the substrate influences, whether in the Mantra dialect or in the vernacular Vedic dialect were considered a normal feature and there was no conscious attempt to prevent these influences. This is evident from the fact that the substrates are not confined to the Old Vedic language, but rather they continue to occur in good measure in the Middle Vedic language as well. The substrate elements may also have entered the Mantra dialect by way of compositions undertaken by Prākṛt- or Dravidian-speaking poets with inadequate training in that dialect. Understanding for a while that the Vedic dialect was the first language of its poets, there would be little scope for substrates from any of the spoken dialects. But in case Prākṛt or Dravidian was the first language of the poets, substrates from these dialects would be a matter of asking.

In a linguistic scenario dominated by spoken dialects and the absence of scripts, great care had to be taken for orally codifying and regimenting the rules of phonology, etymology and syntax, and where the compositions are in the form of songs or some form of chants, the science of metre also received importance. Such care must have been taken in relation to all the dialects, though textual evidence of this has survived only in the case of those dialects that were meant to be liturgically frozen to avoid contamination by non-experts. This was fairly evident from the importance attached, in the case of the Vedic dialect, to the six *Vedāngas*, of which four dealt with the science of language.

These four disciplines are phonetics (*sikṣā*), metre (*chanda*), grammar (*vyākarṇa*) and etymology (*nirukta*). Of these, *sikṣā* relates to the science of proper articulation and pronunciation, comprising the knowledge of letters, accents, the use of speech organs and phonetics, especially the laws of euphony peculiar to the Vedic dialect. Similarly, *chanda* relates to the manner of arranging phonemes and morphemes in different ways, *vyākarṇa* to the structural analysis of language and *nirukta* to the derivational explanation of different words. The two remaining disciplines of the *Vedāngas* are *Jyotiṣ* and *Kalp*. *Jyotiṣ*, or astronomy, represents the Vedic calendar, the primary objective of which was to ascertain the most auspicious days of sacrifice. Like *Jyotiṣ*, *Kalp* also related to the ritual aspect of the religion.

Though the *Vedāngas* are named in much later *Gṛhya* books, some awareness of these branches must have existed among the bardic families about the time the early Vedic language was being given the shape in which it appears in the earliest *Samhitā* texts. The motivation of such linguistic skills may have come from pre-existent spoken dialects, which seem to have provided linguistic ingredients in the creation of a new literary and liturgical dialect.

Notes

1. J.G. Shaffer, 'The Indo-Aryan Invasion, Cultural Myth and Archaeological Reality', in *The Biological Anthropology of India, Pakistan, and Nepal*, ed. J.R. Lukacz, New York: Plenum Press, 1984, pp. 77–88.

2. S. Farmer, J.B. Henderson and M. Witzel, 'Neurobiology, Layered Text and Correlative Cosmologies: A Cross-cultural Framework for Pre-modern History', *Bulletin of the Museum of Far Eastern Antiquities,* vol. 72, 2002, pp. 48–90.
3. M. Witzel, 'Substrate Languages in Old Indo-Aryan', *Electronic Journal of Vedic Studies,* vol. 5, no. 1, September 1999, p. 96.
4. J.G. Shaffer and D.A. Lichtenstein, 'The Concepts of "Cultural Tradition" and "Palaeoethnicity" in South Asian Archaeology', in *The Indo-Aryans of Ancient South Asia: Language, Material Culture and Ethnicity,* ed. G. Erdosy, Berlin and New York: Walter de Gruyter, 1995; repr., New Delhi: Munshiram Manoharlal, 1995.
5. G. Erdosy, 'Ethnicity in the *Ṛigveda* and its Bearing on the Problem of Indo-European Origins', *South Asian Studies,* vol. 5, no. 1, 1989, pp. 35–47.
6. S. Farmer, R. Sproat and M. Witzel, 'The Collapse of the Indus-Script Thesis: The Myth of a Literate Harappan Civilization', *Electronic Journal of Vedic Studies,* vol. 11, no. 2, 13 December 2004, pp. 19–57.

4

Ritual and Power

IN INDIA, LIKE ALL ancient societies, the system of education grew out of the pressing requirements of individuals, families, groups and classes. Depending on the nature of utility, the acquisition, consolidation and dissemination of knowledge was generally homespun and centred round the craft, the commodity, the court and the cult.

For some, like the political and religious elite, the wisdom was inclusive of ideas which could influence the minds of the rest of the population, to fall in line with the political or religious system of a particular time. Knowledge which comes through a system of schooling, formal or informal, is intended to gain prestige in a particular trade or vocation through physical or mental expertise and to obtain power, fame and material benefits in the society. The vocation of priests, who exercised a tight grip over society, was no different. In the realm of the sacred, the basis of such knowledge was the spoken word, articulated in a manner that distinguished it from mundane conversation and involved special communicating skills in the form of accents and intonations in the arrangement of phonemes and morphemes. The vehicle of this wisdom was language which understandably occupied the first spot in the curriculum.

The absence or non-availability of scripted text from the Harappan contexts has lately given rise to speculation that Harappan inscriptions never encoded any form of speech and for that reason there is no question of deciphering the Harappan sign system.[1] It has also been argued that non-linguistic symbols enhance social cohesion among multilingual populations[2] much as has been hypothesized in the case of the radically different types of symbols developed by the Harappans.[3] This means that writing could exist without words and serve as the medium of communication for specified purposes understood universally in a multilingual space. If words were not concomitant to writing, writing too was not concomitant to words of which several varieties existed in the South Asia of the third millennium BC. Creation and circulation of oral texts on religion, politics, musicology, medicine, games and many other subjects would be commonplace in such a scenario both during the third and second millenniums BC though the preservation and transmission of these texts depended on the urgency of their use, like texts of religion, magic and medicine.

The hymns of the *Ṛgveda* that relate to a religious text provide valuable information on related subjects like magic and medicine besides the political system, social life and economic activities. Recent estimates as by Witzel of the chronology of these hymns (see Chapter 3, this volume), though on the conservative side, suggest that the earliest of these compositions go back to the beginning of second millennium BC, with the period of the hymns ranging between 1900 and 1200 BC. The estimates are based on internal data related to genealogies of priests and chiefs and the presumed location of certain linguistic groups in certain areas at given periods of time. The method is far from dependable in the absence of firmly dated historical events and the association of apical ancestors of chiefs and priests with any of these events. By default, the vernacular Vedic dialect that served as the basis of these literary and liturgical creations may easily go back to the middle of the third millennium BC. The substantial nature of Prākṛt, Dravidian and Munda substrates in many of these hymns further identifies the various spoken dialects synchronizing with vernacular Vedic dialects from the mid-third millennium BC if not earlier.

Genesis of the Word

At this point it may be necessary to draw a distinction between the spoken dialects of the Dravidian and primary Prākṛt categories on one hand and the highly-specialized and exclusive liturgical dialect, which could be mastered by persons with high neural motor skills. Such skills would be evident from a cursory look at the Mantra compositions of the *Ṛgveda*. The Mantras not only involved a complex metrical structuring, but also freely incorporated consonantal clusters at the beginning and the end of the words. This is besides the consummate skill in the use of accents, the slightest alteration of which could change the meaning of the word. The articulated morphology of the Mantra dialect appears to have been a guarded preserve of priests and poets well beyond the competence of ordinary individuals. This was not even the common language of its artful composers who used a vernacular form of the Vedic dialect halfway between the Mantra dialect and the primary Prākṛt or Dravidian, but much different from both. The parallel existence of a liturgical Vedic dialect and a colloquial Vedic dialect has been examined at length by some scholars.[4] Attempts to time-freeze the liturgical dialect and articulate a vernacular Vedic language as distinct from the Prākṛt spoken by the common man may already have been evident during the *Ṛgvedic* phase.

The presence of Prākṛt, Munda and Dravidian substrates in the existing *Śākalya* text was surely the result of prolonged bilingualisms involving the speakers of these three dialects who tried to master the Vedic dialect and compose hymns in honour of different divinities. This suggests that as the centre stage of civilization in South Asia, the Greater Indus Valley drew diverse ethno-linguistic communities from different parts of the subcontinent. They became over time an integral part of social, political and religious processes in this region. Since a literary dialect is almost always processed from a widespread spoken dialect, the old Vedic could very well have originated from the primary Prākṛt with substantial lexical and phonological inputs from the Munda and the Dravidian.

The considerable amount of similarity between the Vedic and Prākṛt dialects in the pronunciation of vowels and consonants and use of declensions as well as the nature and extent of Prākṛt substrates in the present *Ṛgveda* also seem to confirm such a possibility. From the lexical point of view, the old Vedic and Primary Prākṛt share a large number of common vocables without any alteration. There are many other vocables which with slight alteration can find place in either dialect. Still other words, exclusive to the Prākṛt dialect, probably did not find acceptance in the Vedic dialect. In case the Vedic dialect was the first language of the authors of different Vedic texts, substrate elements from the Prākṛt would be extremely unlikely. But, if Prākṛt was the first language of those authors, the substrate influences would be a matter of asking. This also applied to Dravidian. The absence of a strict grammatical regimen, the oral nature of composition and transmission and perhaps the insularity of the recensional schools were also partly responsible.

The Prākṛt substrates in the present *Ṛgveda* admit of both the eastern and western varieties in addition to the more dominant north-western variety known as the 'Gāndhāra Prākṛt'. The eastern and western influences point to the literary activism of priests and poets from eastern and western India settled in the Greater Indus Valley rather than to the eastern and western recensions of the *Ṛgveda*. However, the Prākṛt substrates were not confined to the *Ṛgveda*. These continued to occur fairly widely in other *Saṃhitā* texts of the old Vedic dialect as well as the *Brāhmaṇa* and *Āraṇyaka* texts of the middle Vedic dialect. It is difficult to assume that all these authors who were supposedly using their first language to prepare oral texts of great ritual significance frequently succumbed to the influences of a non-literary spoken dialect. These examples perhaps underline the artificial nature of the old Vedic dialect processed from the popular spoken dialects for a limited liturgical purpose.

The pre-eminence of the Dravidian dialect in the Greater Indus Valley and the composition of earliest Vedic or Indo-Aryan poetry in the same region seem to underline some sort of organic relationship between the two dialects. The presence of Dravidian substrates in the Old Indo-Aryan, already noticeable in the *Ṛgveda*, is sufficient evidence of the parallel existence of the two dialects, not much different from one another, lexically as well as structurally. In Tamil, words of Sanskrit origin account for nearly 18 per cent of the vocabulary, but in other languages like Telugu and Kannada, the percentage varies from 50 to 65 per cent. Besides the common use of cerebrals or retroflexed dental consonants, the two dialects share assimilation of stops and pronominal distinction between first-person inclusive plural 'you and I and possibly others' and first-person exclusive plural 'I and others, not you'.[5] The absence of alveolar in the Old Indo-Aryan and the northern Dravidian dialects like Brahui, Malto and Kurukh, and the pre-dominance of alveolar sounds like 'ṭ', 'ḍ', 'ṛ', 'ṣ', 'z' and 'ṇ' in certain Dravidian dialects[6] also points to the fraternal nature of the two dialect families.[7] These dialects also contained words that are not known to any other Dravidian dialects of the south-central, central and southern regions.[8] The importance of cerebrals or retroflexed consonants in Indo-Aryan and the Dravidian and the absence of these sounds in the Iranian and European members of the Indo-European family[9] may suggest the origin of the two former languages from a common indigenous ancestor.

Word and the Ideology

Whatever the linguistic background of the Vedic dialect, the question one needs to address is why the Mantra dialect, meant exclusively for liturgical purposes, should at all have been necessary. It has been suggested on the basis of incisive textual study that the hymns of *Ṛgveda* represented a new religious ideology, that the *Ṛgveda* does not show any evidence of migration from outside South Asia and that important Vedic gods like Indra (and through them the Vedic poets themselves) claimed the land of seven rivers as their own land.[10] Add to this the information relating to urban life, long-distance trade by land and sea, specialized production of craft goods and surplus-oriented, high-end agriculture. This correlation of textual and archaeological data already places the bardic text in a millennium timeline ranging between 2500 and 1500 BC.[11] To understand what an ideology—political, social, religious—is all about and why it was necessary when it came around, one has to look up the text.

The Middle Bronze Age occupies a nodal point in the history of north-western South Asia, Afghanistan, Iran and south Central Asia. This vast territory was inhabited by ethno-linguistic communities with diverse material cultures but strong biological and cultural affinities. The two most important developments of the Middle Bronze Age were persistent and widespread geo-climatic disorder, which struck with vengeance from the close of the third millennium BC, and the degeneration and disintegration of urban and proto-urban civilization over this vast area from about the same time. The degeneration also triggered an internal dynamic that fructified in the shape of new cultural traditions and social reorganization. Many of the old customs and ideas still continued and the pursuit of gainful economic activities surfaced with new dimensions. Older dialects, which occupied marginal space during the urban phenomenon, surged forward and new literary forms were articulated to give expression to the changing experiences of life. These social and cultural trends are as much evident from the late Harappan archaeological record as from the poetic expressions of a people afflicted by persistent catastrophic events. The destabilizing influence of widespread geo-climatic disorder and its social fallout can be deciphered from the archaeological remains of the region. The hymns of the *Ṛgveda*, which give considerable importance to catastrophic events in nature and society and provide a textual corroboration of these events in the archaeological record, also highlight the trauma and misfortune suffered by various groups of people in the Greater Indus Valley.[12]

The reactions and responses to these devastations varied from people to people. Some accepted the misfortune in mute silence while others tried to elevate despondent minds with the promise of divine deliverance and religious practices. Depending on the skills of rote and communication, some were able to preserve and transmit the oral compositions while others virtually lost track of a literary heritage. The skills of preservation and transmission were particularly effective in liturgical circles for reasons of preserving and propagating the newly-developed religious ideology. Two of these dominant liturgical groups were evidently the speakers of the old Vedic dialect and those of the old Avestan dialect.

The *Ṛgveda* is a highly motivated religious text with a traumatic preoccupation with persistent geo-climatic disorders and the resulting civil disturbances, both entailing loss of life and property. No wonder the text is consistently focused on pleasing or placating icons in nature and society, the former for deliverance from a state of utter helplessness, caused by repeated and diverse types of catastrophic events, and the latter for sustenance under such conditions. A classification of historical processes suggested in different portions of the text is, therefore, imperative for historically contextualizing it or its segments. In the *Avesta*, social upheavals occupy a major space and environmental disorders, especially hydrological catastrophes, are alluded to occasionally. This may suggest that Avestan poets, unlike the *Ṛgvedic* bards, lived in an age when natural calamities had become a thing of the past, but the resulting social upheavals continued unabated. This also is in order, since Avestan ideas represent a subsequent breakaway ideology of the *Ṛgveda*.

Also significant is the fact that both the *Ṛgveda* and the *Avesta* are predominantly religious documents motivating people to obey the laws of nature, since transgressions of them were supposed to invite divine wrath in the form of natural disasters and social depredations. The worship of the forces of nature represented by powerful divinities would be only a short step from such a perception of the linkage between human beings and nature. All this possibly relates to an attempted renewal and reinvigoration of human efforts to overcome trauma and integrate as many ethnic groups as possible under the overarching influence of a new religious ideology and supra-local identity.

Word as Oblation

At the earliest stage of bardic interaction with the uninitiated, the whole emphasis was on the spoken word, which was supposed to contain uncanny powers and could, therefore, force the divinity to grant wishes. These early prayers may have meant just a few words or even a few syllables and without metrical regulations to admit phonological variations. Even in the present text, one comes across several words with unaccented syllables. Gradually, as the prayer became a mechanism of control, more and more emphasis was put on metrical regulations. This falls in line with the fact that the chants contained only the Svarit accent in the beginning and that the *Yajurvedic* priests, in a bid to prevent aberrant chants, added the Udātta and Anudātta accents to the *Ṛgveda* mantras. The warning that even the slightest mistake in the proper use of accent would produce just the opposite result further sanctified this.

The conviction that effective poetic compositions (*kavya*), which also served as the oblation (*havya*), sufficed to please the divinity, making fire rituals and oblations redundant, appears to be the guiding principle of bardic exercises. From this angle, the present text of the *Ṛgveda* would appear to be a book of the prayer cult. It is not without good reason that out of over 10,000 invocations recorded in the text only a small number specify the objects of oblation to the fire. The importance of the sacrificial fire, considered to be the carrier of oblations to different Gods, increased with a corresponding decline in the *kavya-havya* (prayer as the oblation) conviction among the bardic people.

The significance of the prayer cult is as much evident from the large number of references to poetic composers in the *Avesta* and the *Ṛgveda* as from the mention of common composers in the two texts. In the *Ṛgveda*, the number of named poets is more than 250 while terms like *kavi* (poet) and *kavya* appear in 240 and 50 passages respectively. The Gathic text was also the work of a large number of poets. To judge from the younger Avestan texts, which mention twenty-seven Kauui composers of the *Gāthās*, the list would have been much longer if a major part of the text had not been lost through careless transmission.

As for the common composers, Uśanā must have been among the earliest bards who received adulation even after the separation of the Avestan and *Ṛgvedic* dialects. The Kauui Uśanā of the Avesta is the same as Kavi Uśanā, or more appropriately, Kavya Uśanā, who figures in about a score of passages in the *Ṛgveda*. Many of these compositions project Kavya Uśanā as the model poet and his compositions as most distinguished poetry by succeeding generations of *Ṛgvedic* bards. The term 'Uśija', which figures in the *Avesta* as well as in the *Ṛgveda*, is also significant. In the Vedic dialect, the term is said to derive from √*vaś*, 'to control, regulate'. The Avestan etymological derivation could not be too far off the *Ṛgvedic* connotation, in view of the fact that in both the bardic traditions, the poet was considered to be the mentor of both gods and people.

Although the earliest bardic prayers were without phonological regimentation and unaccompanied by any fire rituals, considerable concern for the freshness of new compositions is evident. Since the divinities were expected to enjoy the invocations, the repetition of the same material over and over again would be monotonous, and therefore fruitless. At this early stage, the dominant idea was to use the power of prayer to good effect and to articulate a literary style that would be frozen for this purpose. When these verses were chanted with articulate accents before a stranger, the latter was immediately attracted by the power of the sonorous rills emanating from these chants, although he did not understand anything of the whole utterance. A new literary style does not imply that there were many originators. Even single bards gifted with intellect, command over the spoken word and entrepreneurial abilities would suffice to launch such a literary style and for its diffusion to new areas. From this angle, the role of itinerant bards interacting with local chiefs in different parts of the Indo-Iranian subcontinent would become significant.

Word and the Corporate

The inflation of priestly functionaries has an interesting history in the text. The process was gradual rather than sudden and may have covered three distinct stages of development. The first was marked by bardic prayers and unaccompanied by any fire rituals. The next stage marked the introduction of marginal fire rituals, which could be managed by single priests. This single ritualist was the Adhvaryu (*adhvar*, 'sacrifice'), who is regularly mentioned in different portions of the text, the references totalling more than seventy. The Adhvaryu had to measure the ground, prepare the sacrificial vessels, build the altar, fetch wood and water, light the fire, and bring the animals for immolation. While engaging in these duties, he had to repeat the hymns. This bundle of priestly functions was divided up and earmarked for new priestly functionaries like the *Hotā*, the *Potā*, the *Praśāstā*, the *Neṣṭā*, the *Udgātā* and the *Agnidh*.

The *Hotā* (√*hu*, 'to invite') was the priest who called out to divinities to listen to the prayers being uttered for them and receive whatever oblations were made for them. The *Potā* (√*pū*, 'to clean') was expected to purify different objects associated with the fire rituals. The *Agnidh* (√*idh*, √*indh*, 'to fuel and light the fire') priest was the functionary who was entrusted with the responsibility of keeping the flames at a particular level throughout the duration of the sacrifice. The *Udgātā* (*ud* + √*gī*, 'to sing') priest was required to set particular mantras to particular tunes and sing these according to the requirements of the rituals. *Praśāstā* (*pra* + √*śās*, 'to rule') was the functionary who supervised the whole affair from the beginning to the end and was expected to point out lapses on the part of any of the priestly functionaries. The *Neṣṭā* (*nī*, 'to bring forward') was required to ceremonially bring forward the chief and/or the spouse into the sacrificial circle for the legitimation of his or her political authority.

Considering, however, the wide gap in the number of references to Adhvaryu and those to the other functionaries, it is unlikely that the latter functioned on a large scale during the greater part of bardic history. For instance, Adhvaryu appears in over seventy passages of the text, whereas other functionaries taken together do not account for even a third of this number. More importantly, the Adhvaryu dominates every portion of the text, whereas the other functionaries remain confined to particular books. Thus the references to seven priests named here are found in the Second Book, but occasional references to some of these priests are also not wanting elsewhere in the text.

However, the ritualistic phase marked by the Adhvaryu in the *Ṛgveda* witnessed development of a different kind. This related to the introduction of the calendar man or the *Ṛtvij*. The unstated purpose behind the induction of this functionary, who appears in all the portions of the text except the Fourth Book for a total number of sixteen times, was to prescribe and multiply the days and durations of the sacrifice. Probably this is how the number of priestly functions and related functionaries became inflated in the course of time. There are several passages referring to sacrifices continuing for a full year. The year-long sacrifices (*Sāmvatsara*), which are mentioned several times in the text, may have been the handiwork of this functionary.

Word as Commodity

The bardic composer, who moved from one place to another in the course of bardic enterprise, mobilizing patronage from new customers of Vedic ideology and collecting huge gifts of mobile assets, also freely participated in the exchange processes prevalent at the time. In the initial stages, the distinction between the bard and barterer paled into insignificance. While many of the bards were good at trade, some of the traders were also not too unfamiliar with the bardic praxis. Occasionally, the bard may have been a member of the caravan, while at other times someone belonging to the caravan acted as a profound bard. Whether bard or trader, neither thought of a permanent residence for reasons of professional promotion. But both were conscious of increasing the accumulation of goods and speedily disposing them off through barter or money transaction. The only difference between the two was that the former acted as a missionary of new ideology, which was also a selling point in the accumulation of wealth. Although, the constant journey of bardic missionaries facilitated commodification of the gifts and their exchange with locals en route in return for other goods, the task of propagating Vedic ideology prevented the bard from moving out of the new destinations as quickly as the traders.

In the old-world conditions of cultural fluidity and frequent paradigm shifts, the bardic ideology, which involved invocations to different divinities and marginal fire rituals and which promised enhancement of material goods and temporal power, may have found many enthusiastic takers among ethnic South Asians, most of whom were passing through a traumatic phase following the decay of Harappan civilization.

With its characteristic phonology, morphology and manner of reciting, the mantric lore was the guarded preserve of the priest's mental skill. It was unintelligible and mystical to the locals and inspired a sense of awe and reverence towards the priest and his compositions. However, the divinities expected to listen to these invocations and grant the wishes were all too familiar to the locals everywhere. Consider who were to be invoked: the Earth, the Sky, the Rivers, the Sun, the High Seas, the Medicine Man, the Dawn, the Dusk, the Rains, the Storm, the successful

Leader and so on. And what was to be prayed for? Wealth and fame, happiness and longevity, children and subjects, livestock and grains, protection from diseases, protection from predators and protection from calamities.

If bardic prayers could usher in all this, already a tall order, the local chieftain would be only too willing to offer the priest subsistence, security and a place in his entourage. If things went wrong, the blame could always be laid at the door of the chief, on shortcomings in arrangements and provisions or misdemeanour on the part of some unnamed person in the entourage. If things went right, it only fattened the priest and increased his authority. Occasional hiccups in some cases were not unlikely. But the entrepreneurs of priestly craft were gifted enough to overcome such minor tiffs.

This gives an indication how many selling points the poets were trying to score by perfecting a system of chants with the help of attractive vocables, permutation of accents and intonation, application of melody and, finally, soulful rendering. It is not known whether the five modes of saying prayers had already been articulated during the early stages of the prayer cult. But, considering that the power of the prayer mattered most under the given conditions, attempts to develop these methods of recitation may not have been unlikely. The more complex the method of chants was, the greater the efficacy of the utterance and the influence of the person concerned. Though the chants were intended to please or placate different divinities, their greater purpose was roping in of affluent customers in the political and commercial circles. The more munificent the gifts made by these customers were, the more eulogistic the *dānastuti*, or praises sung in honour of the donor and his charities.

However, the praise of gifts was not merely intended to sanctify the donor's political authority. It was also intended to publicize such authority in the court of another chief. This provoked the other chief to outmatch the gifts made by the former donor. It also occasionally provoked hegemonic conflicts between two or more chiefs to fight out a legitimacy crisis. From this angle, the *dānastuti* passages are as much a praise of gifts by the donor as it is of the composer himself.

Word as the Basis of Conflict

Bardic attempts to monopolize priestly authority at the political centres may have occasionally been influenced by ethnic considerations. This is logical, since the bardic composers were drawn from different ethnic groups, irrespective of physical features, dialects and lifestyles. As such there could be fair-skinned bards as well as dark-skinned poets. Kaṇva—who is described as 'Kṛṣṇa' and 'Śyābah', meaning 'dark-skinned', in quite a few passages of the text—appears to have been a victim of ethnic discrimination. A passage of the Tenth Book (10.31.11), which, too, describes Kaṇva as 'Śyābah' and 'Kṛṣṇa', states that no other divinity except the fire god Agni extended patronage to the priest and that the fire god became radiant and caused the Udders or sources of wealth to overflow for Kaṇva.

Apart from ethnic considerations, professional jealousy and the desire to appropriate all the gifts and customers in a particular locality embittered social and political relations in the concerned area and even across the localities. The observations of the bard sound like those of the dealers in a marketplace trying to attract the largest number of customers. This is the precise import of passages in which the poets implore the gods (or chiefs) to denounce priests at other sacrifices and come to those that they themselves perform (8.33.14, 8.66.12, 2.18.3).

The introduction of Soma oblations appears to have further intensified the infighting. In many quarters, the Soma sacrifice was supposed to be more appealing to the gods and therefore more beneficial to the priests and their political patrons. Accordingly, a distinction was made between those who made Soma offerings and those who did not (4.25.6, 4.25.7, 5.34.5). Even those groups that were familiar with the Soma plant but did not make Soma offerings were sought to be sidelined (6.41.4). Damnation was also reserved for those sacrificers who were friendly to bad people, made false display of their wealth and publicized vanity by decorating their bodies (5.34.3). Since Soma offerings would provide benefits to whichever priests made these oblations, the space for gift-sharing narrowed, with diminishing returns to competing priests. The desire to edge out a rival priest from the Soma sector would be natural. An alibi was not far to seek. Soma juice prepared carelessly and/or offered without proper chants would suffice to discredit and disentitle the concerned group (6.41.4, 7.26.1).

Judging by the accounts of Trita and *Kavaṣa*, Soma-related conflicts soon reached a crescendo. Trita was an epical Soma oblator of the *Ṛgvedic* and the Avesthan tradition who enjoyed considerable leverage on account of his newly-developed expertise in the extraction and offering of Soma drink to different gods (2.34.14). But it was the same expertise and the attendant high position that proved to be his undoing and led to his eventual expulsion from the endic homeland. The fact that in the Avesthan tradition Trita ranks next only to Vivasvān (Avesthan Vivangvan) would suffice to suggest that following his humiliation, Trita escaped to Avesthan circles in eastern Iran, which is also confirmed by his reference to Persians (*parśavaḥ*) tormenting him like co-wives (1.105.8). The mention of oppression caused by co-religionists (Stotāraḥ) would also suffice to indicate that it was the rival priests in the Indic homeland who humiliated the poet and forced him to leave the country (1.105.7). The laments over the loss of righteousness and the lack of Varuṇa's surveillance over good and bad people in the Indic homeland shows that the behaviour of *Daiva* worshippers on the Indo-Iranian subcontinent had reached a flashpoint and needed a strong reformist movement to neutralize it (1.105.6).

The reference to Persians in these compositions underlines the fact that the majority of Iranians during the early second millennium BC were followers of either the *Daiva* priests (the Deuus of Avesta) or followed some local religious beliefs. The laments of Trita expressed in these passages resemble the outcry of Zarathuṣṭra against competing groups of *Daiva* worshippers, who did not subscribe to the Ahuric doctrine of monotheism.

The Persian tormentors of *Daiva* worshippers surface once again in the composition of Kavaṣa Ailuṣa, an important poet of the eighth and the tenth book. Like Trita, this composer also refers to the Persians tormenting him like co-wives (10.33.2) and the mental agonies devouring him like the mice eating up tentacles (10.33.3). The passages may be an adoption of previous compositions or these may reflect the actual hostilities experienced by Kavaṣa Ailuṣa in Iran. But, unlike in the case of Trita, the humiliation of Kavaṣa Ailuṣa at the hands of fellow priests had a social angle as well. This social angle is underlined in the *Aitareya Brāhmaṇa*, which belongs to the *Ṛgveda* and almost synchronized with the redaction time of the bardic text. In the Aponaptriya section of the *Aitareya Brāhmaṇa*,[13] the basis of this humiliation seems to be the low birth of Kavaṣa, who is denounced as the son of a slave woman, a cheat and a non-Brāhmaṇa. Considerable anguish and surprise are expressed at the presence of Kavaṣa in the midst of those rightfully making the sacrifices. Those humiliating Kavaṣa debarred him not only from offering Soma oblations but also from inhabiting the banks of Sarasvatī. Kavaṣa was driven to a desert tract where he would be afflicted by thirst and ultimately die. Although, a large part of north-western South Asia had developed into a desert track by 2000 BC, the mention of Persian by Kavaṣa himself and of his ostracism in the desert in the *Aitareya Brāhmaṇa* suggests that the poet and his family could only be assigned to a contiguous region of Iran and Afghanistan.

The passage drops several interesting hints relating to the claims and counterclaims of rival groups of priests. Although such rivalry goes back to the days of the *Ṛgveda*, there is no indication of high or low birth being considered as the basis of priestly entitlement, but with the division of the Arya community into professional groups of priests, warriors and producers together with the entourages of slaves and non-kin labourers, ideas relating to high and low people within the Arya order must have been striking deeper roots. The consignment of Dāsas to a lowly position within the Arya order is already noticeable in certain portions of the bardic text and it is likely that children born in Dāsa families were being increasingly discriminated against and sidelined in every sphere of life.

Word and the Subaltern

Together with the considerations of high and low people, this passage of the *Aitareya Brāhmaṇa* also emphasizes emerging ideas relating to pure and impure regions, to be inhabited by the high-born and the low-born respectively. This has the effect of saying that since Kavaṣa Ailuṣa was a low-born and a non-Brāhmaṇa, he could not drink the water of the Sarasvatī, meaning that he could not live on the banks of the river any longer and must go away to some inhospitable region, like the desert. This may be an early indication of ethno-genetic formations based on purity of life and habitat, which is so characteristic of later Brahmanical ideas.

The descendants of Kavaṣa are however treated differently in the *Kauṣītaki Brāhmaṇa*, which too belonged to the *Ṛgveda*, but post-dated the *Aitareya Brāhmaṇa* by a couple of centuries, coinciding perhaps with the Upaniṣads and *Śatpatha Brāhmaṇa*. True to the spirit of the time the *Kauṣītaki Brāhmaṇa* acknowledges Kavaṣa as a rightful priest and does not use any invectives for him. However, the Kāvaṣeya or the descendants of the Kavaṣa family had come a long way from the days of their humiliations and set themselves firmly on the path of a protest movement. These sentiments are very well reflected in the *Āraṇyakas* and the Upaniṣads. In the *Aitareya Āraṇyaka* (3.2.6),[14] Kāvaṣeyas are seen as straightaway denouncing the study of the Vedas and performance of sacrifices as useless actions. In the *Maitrāyaṇī* and *Kauṣītaki Upaniṣads*, the condemnation is more severe as the study of the Vedas is called *Avidyā* or false knowledge.

As in the case of Soma-related conflicts, the familiarity of certain priests with therapeutic knowledge and the prestige it brought to them was the cause of great concern for those priests who did not possess the knowledge. It is clear enough that neither Bhiṣag Atharvan, the promoters of knowledge relating to health and healing, nor Ghora Āngirasa, the advocates of magic and miracle, were granted the same prestige as that enjoyed by the *Udgātā* hymn-singers, the Adhvaryu fire-ritualists and the Soma oblators and, accordingly, the oral literature developed by these two streams of knowledge were not given the status of revealed knowledge. Thus, it may have become imperative for both Bhiṣag Atharvan and Ghora Āngirasa to organize a sect and fight for a rightful place in the Vedic circle.

It was probably humiliation and ill-treatment like this that brought diverse groups of subaltern priests and composers together. They now belonged to the subaltern ranks together facilitating common prestation interests on ideological counterpoint. The programmes and ideology of these peoples are fairly well-reflected in *Atharvan Āngirasa*, the name by which the *Atharvaveda* was originally known. The expression 'Atharvan Āngirasa' combined two parallel but mutually complementary programmes, one, health and healing (Bhiṣag Atharvan) and the other magic and miracle (Ghora Āngirasa). Taken together, the two programmes exercised a strong influence on the minds of the masses, which is why perhaps the programmes, or rather, their promoters, came in for such severe denunciation. In many portions of the *Ṛgveda* itself, one can notice hostility of this nature, like in the conflict of Indra and Aśvins relating to a secret, healing knowledge and in the decapitation of Dadhīchi, a descendant of Atharvan, in this connection. From the materialistic position of healers and magicians in the *Atharvan Āngirasa*, it was not too difficult for the promoters of these programmes to launch a tirade against the authority of the Vedas as revealed knowledge and mobilize intellectual opinion in favour of anti-Vedic thoughts and movements.

This was brought into fuller relief by later Vedic texts, the Brāhmaṇas, the Āraṇyakas and the Upaniṣads. The Gopatha

Brāhmaṇa, which belongs to the *Atharvaveda*, relates two stories to establish the superiority of the *Atharvaveda* over the *Ṛg*, *Sāma* and *Yajus Saṃhitās*. In the first story, *vāk*, or the divinity of speech, asked all the four Vedas, one by one, to test their ability in taming a wayward mare. The three Vedas—*Ṛg*, *Sāma* and *Yajus*—found that the mare instead of being tamed filled each of them with terror and turned east, west and north respectively at their approach. Finally, all the three Vedas sought the help of Atharvan, who, in his turn, sprinkled the water of tranquillity on the animal, which then calmed down and stood in salutation before the Atharvan. In the other story, the gods asked Indra to protect the sacrifice and find a shelter for the gods. Indra, one by one, took the form of *Ṛg*, *Yajus* and *Sāma* and stood before the gods in the east, west and north respectively to achieve the task. But, each time the gods were dissatisfied. Finally, Indra took the form of the *Atharvaveda* and the gods conceded that now Indra could provide the greatest protection to the gods as well as sacrifices.[15]

Notes

1. S. Farmer et al., 'The Collapse of the Indus-Script Thesis: The Myth of a Literate Harappan Civilization', *Electronic Journal of Vedic Studies*, vol. 11, no. 2, 13 December 2004, pp. 19–57.
2. E.H. Boone and W.D. Mignolo, eds., *Writing Without Words: Alternative Literacies in Mesoamerica and the Andes*, Durham, North Carolina: Duke University Press, 1994.
3. Farmer et al., 'The Collapse of the Indus-Script Thesis'.
4. M.M. Deshpande, *Sanskrit and Prakrit: Sociolinguistic Issues*, Delhi: Motilal Banarsidass, 1993.
5. F.C. Southworth, 'Reconstructing Social Context from Language: Indo-Aryan and Dravidian Prehistory', in *Indo-Aryans of Ancient*

South Asia: Language, Material Culture and Ethnicity, ed. G. Erdosy, Berlin and New York: Walter de Gruyter, 1995; repr., New Delhi: Munshiram Manoharlal, 1995, p. 268 n13.

6. T. Burrow and M.B. Emeneau, *A Dravidian Etymological Dictionary*, Amen House, London: Oxford University Press, 1960, p. 605.
7. Deshpande, *Sanskrit and Prakrit.*
8. M.B. Emeneau, *Brahui and Dravidian Comparative Grammar*, Berkeley: University of California Press, 1962.
9. B. Tikkanen, *The Sanskrit Gerund: A Synchronic, Diachronic, and Typological Analysis, Studia Orientalia 62*, Helsinki: Finnish Oriental Society, 1987.
10. G. Erdosy, 'Ethnicity in the *Rigveda* and its Bearing on the Problem of Indo-European Origins', *South Asia Studies*, vol. 5, no. 1, 1989, pp. 35–47.
11. R.N. Nandi, *Ideology and Environment: Situating the Origin of Vedic Culture*, Delhi: Akaar, 2009, chapters 4–7.
12. Ibid.
13. A.B. Keith, *Rigveda Brahmanas: The Aitareya and Kauṣītaki Brāhmaṇas of the Rigveda*, 1st edn., Cambridge, Mass.: Harvard University Press, 1920; repr., Delhi: Motilal Banarsidass, 1998.
14. L. Swarup, *The Nighaṇṭu and the Nirukta*, 1st edn., 1920, 1927; repr., Delhi: Motilal Banarsidass, 1984.
15. Ibid.

5

Soma in Archaeology and Literature

As THE PRAYER LITURGY spread throughout the Indo-Iranian subcontinent, new elements crept into it. The induction of the Soma cult was one such development. It belonged to certain non-believing ethnic peoples who prepared the juice and consumed it in a ceremonial manner. When these groups were rounded up by the ideology of *Daiva* worship, they incorporated the Soma cult into it. However, before this happened, the ardent practitioners of *Daiva* ideology looked askance at the practice and, even after the induction of the Soma oblations, continued to decry the original practitioners. The original Soma oblators, who were conscious of the importance of Soma offerings in pleasing different divinities, were proud of their expertise and desired a special status within the community of the *Daiva* worshippers. The *Daiva* worshippers, on their part, needed to make Soma offerings to divinities, but were unwilling to concede a corresponding status to newly-assimilated groups of Soma priests. The clubbing together of the Soma invocations in the form of a separate *Maṇḍala* gives some idea of the suggested conflict at the time of the final arrangement of the text. But much more important were the specific instances of rivalry not only between the *Daiva* worshippers and the Soma priests, but also among the Soma oblators themselves.

Aboriginal Beginnings

Originally, Soma appears to have belonged to some dark-skinned ethnic groups, who inhabited the adjoining tracts of the Paropamisas or the Hindu Kush mountains. Unfortunately, no attempt has been made by Vedicists to identify the valley of the river Aṃśumatī, which was the home of this community. In the eighth *Maṇḍala*, we come across the chief of one such community, who ruled on the banks of the river Aṃśumatī and guarded access to the Soma plant. The chief named Kṛśānu was eliminated by Indra together with his fifty dark-skinned wives and army that was 10,000 strong. Later on, however, the so-called demon Kṛśānu, the original keeper of the Soma plant, was turned into a demigod Kṛśānu, the valiant archer, who protected the Soma plant from being stolen by the hawk. Kṛśānu is the same as Keresani of Yaśna IX–X of the *Avesta*, who also performs a similar function.

Archaeological Contexts

The quest of Soma in archaeological contexts would surely involve extensive biochemical analysis of the remains of beverages in the Greater Indus Valley during the third millennium BC, of which no evidence is forthcoming so far. Considering that the ideology of the *Daiva* worship took off in a rural milieu in this area during the decaying phase of Harappan civilization, when the settlements were either deserted or marginalized and the people turning to the countryside for subsistence, archaeologists may perhaps never be able to dig up any evidence of a cultic drink comparable to the *Ṛgvedic* Soma. On the contrary, there are scholars, who would like to situate the ideology and, of course, the Soma cult in the thick of Harappan urbanization, correlating selected items of the Harappan sign system with certain Soma-related verses in the Ṛgveda or even transcribing whole groups of signs into Soma-related verses.[1] The famous *ulukhala* hymn of the first *Maṇḍala* (1.28) comes in for such an exercise. One such attempt draws attention to the correspondence between the *ulukhala* hymn and the signs of a mortar with a flat-bottomed stick inside at a few places, and the same figure with vertical lines issuing from the bottom of the mortar on a few other tablets.[2]

In the *Ṛgveda* (1.28), the term *ulukhala* appears in six of the nine invocations, two of which are addressed to Indra (1.28.1–2), while the remaining four (1.28.3–6) are addressed to *ulukhala* itself. Normally, the poets speak of two stones, probably the saddle and quern for pressing the Soma juice. In the present hymn also, the saddle and quern are mentioned in one passage, although the emphasis seems to be on pressing the Soma twigs in a mortar with the help of a flat-bottomed stick. The importance given to *ulukhala*, a Dravidian term, may suggest that the concerned bards were Dravidian speakers and practised Soma pressing in a mortar instead of saddle and quern. *Ulukhala* signifies a wooden or stone mortar worked with the help of a flat-bottomed stick. In the inscription of two tablets from Harappa, 3309 (H-196) and 3322 (H-227), we find an almost exact replica of the mortar with a flat-bottomed stick.[3] On the reverse of the tablet 3322, the same mortar-like object with a flat-bottomed stick inside it, is marked with four vertical lines issuing from the bottom of the vessel. This is in close agreement with a small, round ivory sculpture with holes at the bottom, probably, representing some sort of strainer recently excavated at Harappa.[4] On tablet 3309, it is carried by a man, as illustrated on many Failaka (Dilmun) seals. The first sign is said to represent the Soma being pressed in the mortar with the help of a flat-bottomed stick. The next sign seems to represent the straining of the Soma juice pressed inside the vessel, while the third sign may signify the distribution of this cultic drink among qualified consumers. Interestingly, the use of a stone mortar and pestle for preparing cultic beverages has been reported from Togolok-21[5] within the Bactria-Margiana archaeological complex of the early second millennium BC.[6]

All this appears quite fascinating although the Soma still remains elusive. In the urban Harappan context, however, the figures could also represent the pounding of grain in mortars, the straining of the pounded grain and its marketing. That the hollow, wooden mortar could have been used for pounding grains has been suggested on the basis of the discovery of husk, barley and wheat found in depressions measuring 0.50 m. in the centre of the brick-laid working floors at Harappa.[7] This seems more logical in view of the fact that the pressing of Soma twigs in the *Ṛgveda* always involved two stones, probably represented by the saddle and quern. The *Ṛgveda* 1.28, which refers to the use of a mortar for extracting Soma juice, may be more of an exception rather than a rule, since the practice is not mentioned anywhere else in the text. Even in this lone hymn, mentioning use of *ulukhala* for Soma pressing, there is a clear reference to the use of a pair of stones for extracting Soma juice (1.28.7).

Unlike the Greater Indus Valley, some evidence of a cultic drink has been reported on the basis of biochemical analysis of the remains of beverages within the Bactria-Margiana archaeological complex. On the basis of available archaeological evidence, the capture of Soma from non-believers and its induction into the *Daiva* worship as a cultic drink may be assigned to the period 1900–1700 BC. In Margiana, ritualistic vessels reported from a temple-like structure are said to contain the organic remains of ephedra. At Gonur-1, the ritualistic vessels also contained remains of poppy and cannabis; at Togolok-21, traces of poppy were found on stone mortars and pestles.[8] Perhaps, none of the three ingredients represented the true Soma of the *Ṛgveda* or Avestan Haoma, though the practice of offering ritualistic drinks to different divinities may not be ruled out.

The Plurality of Soma

From a comparison of the effects of ephedra, poppy and cannabis,[9] it would appear that cannabis could have been the most likely candidate of the *Ṛgvedic* Soma or the Avestan Haoma. But, even the cannabis could produce different effects when prepared differently. The *Ṛgveda* bears testimony to the fact that different bardic peoples prepared the Soma in different ways. Some mixed it with milk (Gavāsīr: 1.137.1, 2.36.1, 2.41.3, 3.32.2, 3.42.1, 3.42.7, 8.52.10, 8.101.10), some with sour milk or curd (Dadhyāsīr: 1.5.5, 1.137.2, 5.51.7, 7.32.4), and yet others with barley flour (*Yavāsīr somam*, 2.22.1). Compared to this, the Soma oblators represented in the ninth *Maṇḍala* always used honey (9.17.8, 9.86.48, 9.97.11, 9.103.3, 9.109.20) and perhaps also milk to prepare the Soma juice. The use of honey gave a reddish-brown colour to the liquor. Interestingly, all the references to a sweetened Soma juice and its reddish colour appear in the ninth *Maṇḍala*. The reddish colour is represented by terms like *Babhru* (9.33.2, 9.63.4), *Hari* (9.3.9, 9.7.6), *Aruṇa* (9.40.2, 9.45.3), *Aruṣa* (9.61.21) and *Śoṇa* (9.97.13). Perhaps, it was the Soma prepared in this manner that sharpened the intellect, increased insight, created joyfulness and enhanced physical strength, thereby qualifying a person to undertake the deepest mental exercises and strenuous physical work. A composer of the sixth *Maṇḍala*, who may have been associated with the original home of the Soma oblations in Afghanistan, bears testimony to the invigorating nature of the drink when he states that 'on drinking Soma, our speech became powerful and intellect became sharpened' (6.47.3, 6.47.5).

For a tentative identification of the abode of the Soma plant, we may turn to the relevant passages in the *Ṛgveda* and the *Avesta*. In several passages of the former text, Soma is said to have been found on Mount Mujavant. In another passage, reference is made to Munj, which together with several types of grasses and reeds served as the hiding place for serpents. Muja or Munj may have been a type of grass or reed, which grew thick on a mountain of that name which was the abode of Soma. In the Fraberdin Yast of the Great Yasts, Muja is mentioned with several other places as the settlements of Ahura worshippers who also incorporated Soma offerings in their liturgy.

Muja, which is located by some scholars in the adjoining region of the Hindu Kush and the Pamirs, may be the same as the Mujavant of the *Ṛgveda*. In Yasna IX–X of the *Avesta*, Baga, who appears to be the same as the *Ṛgvedic* god Bhaga, is stated to have planted the Soma on the top of a mountain. Clearly, there is no doubt about the mountainous home of the plant. Later on, its plantations may have spread to other areas of South Asia and Iran, particularly in the foothills and the adjoining plains. The planting of Soma on the top of a mountain by Baga may have been later on identified as the plant of Baga. With permissible nasalization, Baga soon became Banha of the *Avesta* and Bhang of the *Atharvaveda*. Yasna IX also refers to two types of the plant, one white and the other yellow. Detailed paleo-botanical studies may help to identify the two varieties of the Soma plant. But, surely Banha or Bhanga (modern Bhāng), which was the later appellation of the original Soma plant, is the only herbal intoxicant which is ground to extricate its juice, mixed with milk and other invigorating substances and is well known among South Asians and Iranians. No such exercise is undertaken in relation to either the poppy or ephedra.

There is a good deal of agreement among scholars that the earliest Indo-Iranians were both the innovators and exclusive consumers of the Soma drink.[10] The term 'Soma' in the *Ṛgveda*, means a god as well as a plant growing on the Mujavant Mountains. But, more frequently it represents the invigorating drink prepared from a variety of substances like milk, honey and extracts of a plant with hallucinogenic or sympathomimetic qualities. The evidence from the Margiana archaeological complex cited here shows that hemp, poppy and ephedra were used by the people of the area to prepare intoxicating drinks during the nineteenth and eighteenth centuries BC.

The hemp plant is a dioecious plant usually considered to be monotypic, although three species—*Cannabis sativa Lam., Cannabis indica Lam., Cannabis ruderalis Janisch*—have been distinguished.[11] The use of hemp preparations (Bhanga) results in an altered, dreamy state of consciousness, with a feeling of well-being and even joy. But cultivation of hemp is not exclusive to mountainous regions. This may suggest that the hemp was not representative of Soma though it may have been one of the important ingredients in the preparation of the cultic drink.

The mountainous home of Soma may point towards either ephedra or red fly agaric (*Amanita muscaria*). As a mycorrhizal mushroom associated with birch, pine and some other conifers in warmer climates, it is found only in mountainous areas.[12] The plants are bushes of variable height (0.2–4.0 m.), with a tree-like twisted trunk and numerous, leafless, green or yellowish stems. Of the forty species, those which grow in mountainous terrain have the highest ephedrine content. The marrow of the stems is either brown or colourless.[13] The brownish marrow is said to be responsible for the greyish-brown (*Babhru*) colour of Soma drinks. Plants of the genus ephedra are leafless, usually dioecious gymnosperms, which have clear sympathomimetic effects on man.[14] The main effects of its use are mood fluctuations from bliss to rage and hallucinations, besides lack of muscular co-ordination and a sense of unreality.[15] The capacity to exceed one's physical powers has also been reported. For superficial observers, this may appear significant in the context of frequent fights for the possession of cattle, agricultural land and water courses in the *Ṛgveda*. However, the effects of ephedra are said to be 'of insufficient intensity' or 'too inconsistent in character'.[16] It can be pharmacologically effective only when consumed occasionally.[17] After pushing a person into over-activity, physically, it causes a severe loss of energy, making it unsuitable for regular consumption. This seems to disqualify ephedra as the true representative of *Ṛgvedic* Soma and Avestan Haoma. As already suggested, the Soma was a healthy and invigorating drink, which was consumed frequently, almost daily and not restricted to solemn occasions as Nyberg thinks. There are references to three offerings of Soma drink every day: in the morning, at mid-day and in the evening. In all likelihood, the Soma was an intoxicating and invigorating drink prepared differently in different areas of the Indo-Iranian subcontinent. Some may have used ephedra, others hemp and yet others poppy. In certain cases, a hygienic combination of more than one of these plants may have been involved. Even today, the preparation of hemp juice in most Indian households requires poppy seeds besides milk, honey and dry fruits.

Ancient Soma Priests

Scanning the Gathic text, it would appear that Soma oblation was incorporated into the Ahuric cult much after the induction of Soma offerings into the *Ṛgvedic* liturgy. This would be clear from the mention of five chief Soma oblators—Vivasvān, Trita, Aithya, Kerasaspa, Pourūṣāspa and Zarathuṣṭra. Zarathuṣṭra, who appears to have been a reformer rather than an originator of the Ahuric faith, received the Soma cult from his father, Pourūṣāspa. Some of these Soma oblators are mentioned along with their descendants, who, taken together, would account for as many as nine Soma-related characters, spanning almost a quarter of a millennium. Despite the mention of descendants in some of the cases, the five chief oblators represented separate lineages of bards, each with its own succession of preachers and timescale, rather than succeeding generations of the same family. Once again, the time covered by these preachers would be considerable, probably a quarter of a millennium or even more.

For suggesting an approximate date of the introduction

of Soma cult into the Mazdian liturgy, one may consider three different pieces of information. First, according to the Zoroastrian tradition, Zarathuṣṭra was born on 26 Ferberdin, 1767 BC. Second, Bactria and its neighbourhood figure prominently in the list of sixteen excellent regions created by Ahura Mazda for the settlement of the Aryas and mentioned accordingly in the Vendidad, chapter one. Third, in situ evidence of a cultic beverage has been noticed within the Bactria-Margiana archaeological complex dateable between 1900 and 1700 BC. Piecing together these bits of information, Zarathuṣṭra may have assumed the leadership of the Ahuric faith and, impressed by the popularity of the Soma drink in certain parts of the Indo-Iranian borderlands, adopted it ceremonially into the Mazdian liturgy.

Coming to individual Soma oblators of the Avestan tradition, we have at least two characters, Vivasvān and Trita, who are common to the *Ṛgveda* and the old *Avesta*. In the *Avesta*, Vivasvān is recognized as the earliest Soma priest followed by Aithya, Trita, Keresaspa and Pourūṣāspa. This would suggest a considerable amount of time intervening between the lineage of Vivasvān and that of Trita. Contrary to this, Vivasvān and Trita, who appear in a large number of *Ṛgveda* invocations as composers and Soma pressers, do not indicate any personal or familial connection, so much so that the two are hardly mentioned together except in one or two passages, which may be a mix-up of unrelated characters by a later composer. However, the association of Vivasvān with Aśvins and Yama as a father may suggest that Vivasvān lived much earlier than Trita. Compared to the Avestan account, the *Ṛgvedic* evidence is varied and time-specific, suggesting different twists in the life of each of the two Soma pressers.

There are other passages in the text that characterize them as divinities, Vivasvān being incorporated into the solar pantheon as the charioteer of the Sun God and Trita as a dweller of the remotest region, keeper of nectar and a destroyer of demons. The two types of allusion clearly underline two widely different periods of time during which ordinary humans with certain extraordinary qualities were elevated to the position of a divinity. In this case, the expertise of Vivasvān and Trita in Soma oblation was viewed with considerable respect by subsequent generations of bards, who raised them to the position of divinities. The text of the *Ṛgveda* is replete with such time-deep pieces of information, which can be used to good effect for an internal stratification of 10,000-odd compositions.

Both Vivasvān and Trita may have been already familiar with the Soma plant, its whereabouts and its efficacy as a powerful drink. Accordingly, they may have induced their *Daiva*-worshipping friends to obtain the plant from an ethnic non-believing community. As originators of the Soma cult among *Daiva* worshippers, Trita enjoyed a special position for quite some time. Interestingly, in four passages of the ninth *Maṇḍala*, which is a Soma book, Trita is praised as offering Soma to the Gods (9.32.2, 9.34.4, 9.37.4, 9.38.2). In one passage of the *Ṛgveda*, he even assumes the guardianship of *Daiva* worshippers, inviting five leading priests (*Pañca Hotṛn*, 2.34.14) to be under his protection and patronage. However, with the passage of time, rivalry between different groups of bardic composers increased and each group tried to outwit the other. In such a situation, the Soma oblators were conspicuous objects of envy. This is very well-suggested by the story in the *Ṛgveda* relating to Trita, Ekta and Dvita.

Trita was once travelling with his two brothers Ekta and Dvita. The two greedy brothers, desirous of Trita's property, pushed him into a well while he was drawing water from it. The well was then shut with a wheel. Shut up in the well, Trita composed a hymn to God and worked a miracle to prepare the Soma, so that he may drink it and offer it to God for rescue (1.105.17). The miraculous power associated with Soma offerings and the prestige it gave to the oblators in the eyes of affluent supporters soon became a matter of jealousy for other groups of priests. Some of these detractors, contemporary or slightly subsequent, tried to humiliate the originators of the Soma-cult by assigning them to the remotest regions of the world, where people wished to drive away calamities: 'The sins, which are known (*yat āvi asti*), the sins, which have been committed secretly (*yat duṣkṛtaḥ apicyaṃ*), may all those go to the realm of Trita Āptya, may these go away for me' (8.47.13); 'O daughter of the day (dawn), the bad dreams, which appear in the cow stalls and in me (i.e. in my sleep), may these be dispatched for (the abode of) Trita Āptya' (8.47.14); 'O daughter of the day (dawn), the bad dreams, which haunt the jeweller/goldsmith (Niṣka) and the florist (Srajaḥ)—All those may be dispatched to the realm of Trita Āptya' (8.47.15); 'O Ūṣā! All the bad dreams of the consumer of food, performer of duties are the share of Trita' (8.47.16). In historical terms, all this may signify the migration of a group of Soma oblators to adjoining parts of Iran and Afghanistan, where Trita became one of the apical Soma oblators among the followers of Ahura Mazda.

However, misfortune continued to follow this apical Soma oblator even into Iranian territory. Trita Āptyah, who composed an important Sūkta of the first *Maṇḍala* provides a graphic description of what happened to him during the early years of his emigration to the Persian country. To quote the bard, 'it was I who prayed at the ancient Soma cult, but my tormentors are eating me up as the wolf devours a thirsty deer' (1.105.7); 'the Persians are tormenting me like the jealous co-wives' (*parsavah mā abhitaḥ sapatnyaḥ iva samtapanti*), 'my rival worshippers are causing me agony like a rat eating the tentacles' (*mūṣhāh Śiśna na te stotāram māadhyaḥvi adanti*, 1.105.8). 'Where has righteousness disappeared, where is Varuṇa's surveillance and where is the great path of Aryamā by which we can destroy the wicked' (1.105.6). The Persian tormentors of *Daiva* worshippers surface once again in the composition of *Kavaṣa Ailuṣa*, an important poet of the eighth and the tenth book. Like Trita, this composer also refers to the Persians tormenting him like co-wives (10.33.2) and the mental agonies devouring him like the mice eating up tentacles (10.33.3). The passages may be an incorporation of previous compositions or these may reflect the actual hostilities experienced by *Kavaṣa Ailuṣa* in Iran. The clear reference to Persians in these compositions underlines the fact that the majority of Iranians during the early second millennium BC were followers of either *Daiva* priests (the 'Deuus' of *Avesta*) or followed some local religious beliefs. The laments of Trita expressed in these passages resemble the outcry of Zarathuṣṭra against competing groups of *Daiva* worshippers who did not subscribe to the Ahuric doctrine of monotheism.

Notes

1. E. Richter-Ushanas, *The Indus Script and the Ṛgveda*, Delhi: Motilal Banarsidass, 1997, p. 51.
2. Ibid.
3. Ibid.

4. R.H. Meadow and J.M. Kenoyer, 'Harappa Excavations 1993: The City Wall and Inscribed Materials', in *South Asian Archaeology*, ed. A. Parpola and K. Koskikallio, 1993 repr., Helsinki: Suomalainen Tiedeakatemia, 1994, p. 467.
5. A. Parpola, *Deciphering the Indus Script*, 1994; repr., Cambridge: Cambridge University Press, 1997.
6. V.L. Sarianidi, 'Southwest Asia: Migrations, the Aryans and Zoroastrians', *Information Bulletin of the International Association for the Study of the Cultures of Central Asia*, vol. 13, 1987, pp. 44–56; S. Kussov, '"White Rooms" in the Temples of Margiana', *New Studies in Bronze Age Margiana, Information Bulletin of the International Association for the Study of the Cultures of Central Asia*, vol. 19, ed. F. Hiebert, Moscow: Nauka, 1993, pp. 128–35.
7. A. Ghosh, ed., *An Encyclopaedia of Indian Archaeology*, vol. 1, Indian Council of Historical Research, New Delhi: Munshiram Manoharlal, 1989, pp. 81, 316.
8. Sarianidi, 'Southwest Asia'; Kussov, '"White Rooms" in the Temples of Margiana'.
9. H. Nyberg, 'The Problem of the Aryans and the Soma: The Botanical Evidence', in *The Indo-Aryans of Ancient South Asia: Language, Material Culture and Ethnicity*, ed. G. Erdosy, Berlin: Walter de Gruyter and Co., 1995; repr., 1st Indian edn., Delhi: Munshiram Manoharlal, 1997, chapter 16.
10. Ibid.
11. R.E. Schultes and A. Hofmann, *The Botany and Chemistry of Hallucinogens*, 1995; repr., 2nd edn., Springfield: Charles C. Thomas, 1997.
12. Nyberg, 'The Problem of the Aryans and the Soma'.
13. H. Falk, 'Soma I and II', *Bulletin of the School of Oriental and African Studies*, vol. 52, no. 1, pp. 77–90; P. Martens, *Les*

Gnetophytes, vol. 2, Handbuch der Pflanzenanatomie XII, Berlin: Gebruder Bomtraeger, 1971, p. 24.

14. K.K. Chen and C.F. Smith, 'Ephedrine and Related Substances', *Medicine*, vol. 9, 1930, pp. 1–117; R. Hegenauer, *Chemotaxonomie der Pflanzen*, vol. 1, Basel: Birkhauser Verlag, 1986, pp. 547–51.
15. A. Bresinsky and H. Besl, *Giftpilze: Ein Handbuch für Apotheker Artzte und Biologen*, Stuttgart: Wissenschaftliche Verlagsgesellschaft, 1985, pp. 98, 102.
16. D.S. Flattery and M. Schwartz, *Haoma and Harmaline: The Botanical Identity of the Indo-Iranian Sacred Hallucinogen 'Soma' and its Legacy in Religion, Language and Middle Eastern Folklore*, Berkeley: University of California Press, 1989, p. 72.
17. Nyberg, 'The Problem of the Aryans and the Soma'.

6

Revisiting the Sarasvatī

A PERUSAL OF HYDRONYMS in the *Ṛgveda* would show that the Sarasvatī was the only river which drew the largest number of prayers from bardic composers who described it as the Supreme Goddess (*devītame*), Supreme Mother (*ambitame*) and the Supreme River (*nadītame*). Such appellations would not have been used for a dried-up river. The river Sarasvatī, which rises in the Siwaliks, nearly dries away after covering a distance of 200 km. from the hills. Studies based on remote sensing have brought to light the paleo-channel (the present Ghaggar-Hakra) of the river, which stretched up to the Arabian Sea and had settlements all along the route. This falls in line with a stanza that describes the river as protecting people inhabiting fortified settlements along its banks (*āyasīḥ pūḥ*, 7.95.1). The *Ṛgveda* also describes the Sarasvatī as flowing all the way from the hills to the sea. It is generally believed that the once mighty river, which has changed its course at least four times over the past several thousand years, finally lost its track in the deserts of Rajasthan. The event coincided with a flashpoint in the hyper-arid episode of the Holocene Era about the beginning of the second millennium BC, 2000–1900 BC to be precise. A large part of *Ṛgvedic* hymns, including those addressed to the Sarasvatī, were composed well before this date. There is no suggestion in the *Ṛgveda* of the disappearance of the mighty river, which one would normally expect. But the large number of passages devoted to it, the so-called nature myths, bear testimony to what was happening in the Greater Indus Valley about the beginning of the second millennium BC.

The name 'Sarasvatī', or praise of it, appears in as many as fifty-two invocations of the *Ṛgveda* and, with a few exceptions, the invocations almost invariably glorify a goddess, sometimes a river goddess and sometime later as a goddess of speech (*vāk*). Most important of these are the fourteen stanzas addressed to the river goddess Sarasvatī in the Sixth Book (6.61.1–14). Compared to this, there are nine invocations to river Indus and its eastern tributaries (10.75.1–9). Though the river Indus is glorified as one whose banks are enriched by excellent chariots, horses, textiles, hemp and woollen products, there is no suggestion of it being projected as a divinity. The eastern tributaries of the Indus mentioned in this hymn include Sutlej which, together with the Beas, finds prominent focus in an entire hymn of the Third Book (3.33.1–13). Despite high-decibel praise heaped on these two rivers, there is no indication of their being treated as a divinity. The western Sarasvatī, situated in Afghanistan, comes in for a simple mention in three stanzas, without any praise.

A close examination of the passages relating to the river Sarasvatī reveals a wide divergence of time and space. Though most invocations are characteristic of the time when the great river was in full flow, very few underline a period when the river was drying up, forcing people to leave its banks in search of a new habitat. Also, while most of the passages relate to the eastern Sarasvatī, represented by the dry Ghaggar-Hakra River of today, there are very few passages which refer to the western Sarasvatī, the Haraxvaity of the *Avesta* and the Harauti of the Old Persian inscriptions.

Yet another aspect of invocations to the Sarasvatī underlines varying roles assigned to the river or the river goddess in different portions of the text. Of the fifty-two passages referring to Sarasvatī, more than half suggest a powerful river, which nourished people living on its banks. There are, however, some other passages in which the river goddess appears in the company of Bhāratī and Ilā to constitute a triad of Āprī deities. In these passages, the name 'Sarasvatī' seems to represent the goddess of speech probably because it also flows like the river, both with their characteristic resonance. Interestingly, these invocations generally appear either in the First or in the Tenth Books.

There are still other passages in which the Sarasvatī becomes almost identical with a river of the after-life, like the Vaitaraṇī, which every departed soul was obliged to negotiate. These invocations, which appear in the funerary portions of the text (10.17), implore the river goddess to accompany the departed soul on its forward journey or to take her seat in the company of the departed ancestors on the southern side of the sacrificial ground. It would be incorrect to mess up all these compositions together, as the redactors of the present text have already done, and pass them as the work of just one period, one community and one culture.

For a beginning, one may have a good look at the various descriptions of the river, particularly in the Sixth and the Seventh Books. In the Sixth Book, there is a full hymn of fourteen invocations (6.61) address to the Sarasvatī. In the Seventh Book, there are altogether ten invocations in two hymns (7.95 and 7.96) addressed to the Sarasvatī and Saraśvan. The mention of 'Saraśvan' in association with Sarasvatī is significant in view of the fact that the Saraśvan of these passages represents the sea and that the connection between the river and the sea is mentioned in quite a few invocations of the Sixth and the Seventh Books. Sarasvatī also appears in four passages of the Second Book, one of which describes her as *ambitame*, *nadītame* and *devītame*. This is quite in keeping with the mighty ancient river, which laid the foundation of civilization as and when the people in the neighbourhood were ready for it. The only portions of the text that do not contain invocations to Sarasvatī are the Third and Fifth Books.

The river is said to rise in dizzy highlands, break open the stone barriers, cut its channel, and proceed to the sea with a mighty roar (*roruvat carati*). Full of water and with widely separated banks, the river is said to be the best of the seven sisters, meaning probably the seven major rivers from the Indus on the west to the Ghaggar on the east. In several passages, the river is called 'Vājinivatī', or full of resources. It protects the people living on its banks like a large tree protecting birds. People approach the river and salute it on bent knees, seeking protection and wealth. Time and again, the bards pray to the river to give them wealth and security. It bestows on its people two types of wealth (*ubhe andhasi*). The two types of wealth may relate to the crops grown on the floodplains of the river and the merchandise brought in through navigation. The procurement of goods through river trade and coastal navigation is further stressed by a passage of the Seventh Book, which refers to enterprising people approaching the sea for this purpose. There is an interesting passage in the Seventh Book (7.96.6), which describes the sea as 'Viśvadarśatah', or connecting all lands and its waves carrying goods from one region to another. The description of the river Sarasvatī as 'Ratnadhā' (1.164.49) and 'Marūtsakhā' (7.96.2) may fall in line in this context. Having Marūts, or trade winds, as friends clearly underlines their importance in the movement of cargo boats along the river and cargo ships on the high seas. Different aspects of river navigation and seafaring activities mentioned in the text have been discussed elsewhere.[1]

The description of the river Sarasvatī as a mighty river full of water with widely separated banks seems to be confirmed by a new study[2] which pushes the beginnings of the Harappan civilization to 7000 BC and speaks of heavy to very heavy annual precipitation between 7000 and 5000 BC. Using a technique called 'optically stimulated luminescence' to date pottery shards, the investigators have dated the Early Mature Harappan phase to 4000 BC and a pre-Harappan Hakra phase to 6000 BC. Analysing the oxygen isotope composition in the mammal bones and teeth phosphates, the investigators concluded that monsoon was much stronger between 7000 and 5000 BC, feeding the rivers and making them mightier, with vast floodplains. Even the weakening of the monsoon did not matter much as the Harappans sailed through the Mature phase into the thick of mid-Holocene hyper-arid conditions by suitably adjusting crop patterns according to climate change and replacing large granaries with small household grain stores.[3]

There are two passages in the Seventh Book that deserve special attention in this connection. One of these passages invokes the protection of the river, which can match the strength of masonry settlements (*āyasīḥ pūḥ*) of some kind. Some of the settlements along the river were probably enclosed habitations, the enclosure being made of bricks, mud-bricks or stones. During the high floods, when the countryside was inundated, it was some of these walled settlements that continued to exist and battle with the floods. This may have been the landscape towards the close of the third millennium BC when many of the Harappan settlements were already deserted and others in a precarious state of existence, architecturally as well as culturally.

As the mass of bardic material on the river Sarasvatī cannot be washed away, it has to be accepted that these passages were composed at different periods and in different localities of the Ghaggar-Hakra Valley during the third millennium BC. The people who sang the glory of a mighty ancient river also lamented its depletion and disappearance at a later date. The present river, which originates in the Siwaliks, begins to dry up only after covering 200 km. At present, the Hakra represents the Pakistani part of the Sarasvatī, which passes through the Cholistan Desert and is completely dry. On the other hand, the Ghaggar represents the Indian part of the Sarasvatī, which retains water for a major part of the year.

Things were quite different during the late fourth and early third millennium BC when the river was fed by two mighty streams on its either side, the Yamunā on the east and the Sutlej on the west, both originating in the massive Himalayan glaciers. Fortunes began to fluctuate about the middle of the third millennium BC and, in the course of a few centuries, the ancient Sarasvatī had almost disappeared from the hydrographic map of this region. Such a climax may have taken place any time after 2100 BC. Bardic laments to this effect are not also wanting. The last passage (6.61.14) of the Sarasvatī hymn in the Sixth Book underlines what may have happened to the once prosperous people of the river Ghaggar-Hakra. The poet implores the river not to inundate its banks, threaten its people and drive them away to distant places. Evidently, in this case, people were migrating not because of the desiccation of the river but because of its frequent, unpredictable floods. It is possible that the river, which runs through flat terrain, may have been frequently changing its course during the mid- and late third millennium BC, disturbing the floodplains every now and then and dispersing people in all directions.

According to one estimate,[4] the river Ghaggar-Hakra received its first setback around 2500 BC as a result of some tectonic activity. This may have resulted in the Sutlej (Śutudri) shifting its channel from the Ghaggar-Hakra and constituting an independent drainage system together with Beas (Vipāś) and discharging into the Great Rann of Kutch, which was an ancient extension of the Arabian Sea. This relates very well to a hymn of the Third Book which emphatically characterizes the two rivers as reaching out to the sea (3.33.2–3). The next setback came around 2100 BC when another tectonic lift disturbed the Sutlej system, which moved further west and eventually joined the Indus as we see it at present. About the same time, the Yamunā may also have shifted from the Ghaggar-Hakra drainage to meet the Gangā on the east. At present, the Yamunā is quite far away in the east from the dwindling river Ghaggar in Haryana.

This hydrographic scenario does not fit well with the bardic descriptions of a nearby river called Yamunā. The description of the battle of the ten kings, which was fought on the left bank of the Ravi (Paruṣṇi) includes a reference to the victorious king Sudāsa performing horse sacrifices on the banks of the Yamunā, literally the heads of horses to Indra. Clearly, the Yamunā was far closer to the Ravi Valley in ancient times than it is at present. A passage of the third *Maṇḍala* also sheds some light on the configuration of the drainage of Punjab and Haryana. Two invocations composed by Viśvāmitra refer to the crossing of the Sutlej and the Beas, in that order (3.33.5; 11; 13; 12), on the way to the Ravi to participate in the battle of ten kings. The joint mention of the Sutlej and Beas in this connection and the absence of any mention of the Sarasvatī may suggest that the Sutlej had already deserted the Ghaggar-Hakra and formed its own system together with the Ravi.

The Western Sarasvatī

A word also needs to be said about the Sarasvatī of Afghanistan or the western Sarasvatī. The passages that refer to the western Sarasvatī are very few in number but provide enough hints to distinguish it from its eastern counterpart. The most important divider is the fact that the eastern Sarasvatī is frequently described as rising in the mountains and proceeding all the way to meet the sea. Compared to this, none of the rivers of Afghanistan has any outlet to the sea except the Kabul River, which passes into the Arabian Sea through the Indus. The Argandab, or the ancient Sarasvatī, disappears into the landlocked Helmand Sea just as Harirud (*Ṛgvedic* Sarayu, Avestan Haroiva, Greek Aria) does in the sandy marshes of south Central Asia.

Another marker of the western Sarasvatī is the enumeration of the rivers flowing through Afghanistan and Baluchistan. The eastern Sarasvatī had a direct link with the Indus, but there is no such possibility in the case of western Sarasvatī or the present Argandab. This is precisely what a composer of the Tenth Book seems to signify in two passages of the famous Nadi Sūkta (10.75). The purpose of the two passages is to enumerate the eastern and western tributaries of the Indus. In relation to the eastern tributaries, the order of enumeration is from east to west like the Gangā, Yamunā, Śutudri, Paruṣṇi, Asikni, Vitastā, Marutvṛdhā and Susoma (10.75.5). There is no mention of the Vipāś or Beas, which meets the Sutlej and not the Indus. Similarly, in relation to the western tributaries of the Indus, most of them remain unidentifiable and their enumeration a little erratic, inasmuch as it mentions Sindu itself as a tributary of the Indus (10.75.6). The western tributaries named here are the Tṛṣṭmā, Susartu, Rasa, Sweta, Sindu, Kubha, Gomati, Krumu and Mehatnu. There is no mention of either Sarayu or Sarasvatī. Judging from the accuracy of enumeration of the eastern tributaries, which start with the Gangā, the composer of these passages must have been a native of Upper Gangā Valley, somewhere in western Uttar Pradesh. It is also clear that the passages were composed before the eighteenth century BC, by which time the eastern Sarasvatī or the Ghaggar-Hakra had become almost dry, with no connection either to the sea or Indus.

The western Sarasvatī also figures in two important passages of the Tenth Book (10.64.8–9). One of these passages mentions the Sarasvatī, the Sarayu and the Sindu, each of which was enriched by seven tributaries. The Indus receives more than seven tributaries from the west, but the bard is conscious of the conventional prime number seven in this case. The Sarayu or the Harirud, which flows from east to west, far away from the Indus, also receives seven tributaries, maybe more than seven, during its entire journey of nearly a thousand kilometres. In comparison, the Sarasvatī (Haraxvaity of the *Avesta*) or the Argandab cover only 500 km. before joining the Helmand towards the south-west. The Argandab, too, receives several smaller tributaries on its way to the Helmand.

The Afghan context of the composition and the composer is further evident from the mention of Kṛśānu (*kereshani* of the *Gāthās*), the archer-keeper of the Soma plant, who is invited together with the three rivers named previously, besides the mountains and the forests, to the sacrifice being organized for Rudra. A sacrifice performed in honour of Rudra in Afghan territory is significant inasmuch as Rudra was the father of Marūts or the storm gods. Marūts are praised in about eleven hymns of the Fifth Book by a poet name Śyāvāśva whose travels were also confined to Afghanistan and the neighbouring Pakistan and who seems to be a composer of Iranian origin from the suffix *Aśva* or the Avestan *Aspa* added to his name. The rivers that figure in the account of Śyāvāśva are the Rasa, Anitabhā, Kubha (Kabul), Krumu (Kurram), Sarayu and Sindu. Gomatī (Gomal), another important river of the Pakistan-Afghan borderland, is mentioned in a separate passage. The Marūts in this case may represent the cyclonic winter rains of Mediterranean origin which provide some moisture to the generally arid Afghan country as also other arid regions in the north and north-west of Iran including Armenia. The Hurrians of early second millennium BC may have perceived these storms as a female divinity to be represented by the storm goddess Hepa. Rudra, whose most important trait is to produce a roaring sound (√*rud*, 'to roar'), would thus be an eligible father to the cyclonic wind gods, the Marūts.

As for other indicators, the opening invocation of the Sarasvatī Hymn (6.61) mentions the names of Divodāsa, Vadhṛyāśva and the Paṇis in association with the river Sarasvatī. The association of Divodāsa with Paṇis in this passage and a supposed identification of the Paṇis with Parnians mentioned in the account of Strabo may have prompted[5] Hillebrandt to assign Divodāsa to the western Sarasvatī Valley. Neither of the two suggestions made by Hillebrandt has found much acceptance among Vedicists. The association of Divodāsa with the western Sarasvatī River has been described as improbable by the authors of the Vedic *Index*. Considering that Hillebrandt wrote more than a hundred years ago and that the Vedic *Index* has never been revised after its first publication in 1912, a re-examination of the whole episode may not be out of place.

Divodāsa may have been a Dāha chief of Irano-Afghan origin who ruled in the Sarasvatī Valley. Some sort of political humiliation caused by neighbouring chiefs may have forced Divodāsa to leave his original chiefdom and establish a new one on the banks of the Ravi where his famous descendant Sudāsa won an exemplary victory in the battle of ten kings. Personal names with the 'Aśva' or 'Aspa' suffix are very frequent in the Avestan text, but occur only rarely in the *Ṛgveda*. Two other examples are Śyāvāśva, who is the composer of a large number of hymns in the Fifth Book, and Iṣṭāśva, who is the same as Avestan Viṣṭāśpa, a contemporary of Zarathuṣṭra. In all likelihood, Vadhṛyāśva may have accompanied Divodāsa to his new kingdom in Punjab. His name figures just once in a composition of the Bharadvāja family, which served Divodāsa in his new kingdom. The Afghan home of Divodāsa also seems well-suggested by frequent references to him as the Soma-sacrificer. The original home of the Soma plant was somewhere on the Hindu Kush mountains.

As for the Paṇis, it has already been shown elsewhere[6] that the people bearing this name were separate groups of bankers, barterers and potential stock-breeders of the third millennium BC, some settling at a place and others undertaking long distance journeys by land and sea for trade.

The identification of the western Sarasvatī also seems quite evident from two passages of the Eighth Book, which refer to Citra as the most powerful ruler of the Sarasvatī Valley. The 'Citra' of these passages is the same as 'Citraratha' of the Fourth Book who along with Arṇa was killed by Indra on the banks of the Sarayu. Evidently, there were two rivers named 'Sarasvatī' and 'Sarayu', which were flowing in close proximity for some distance before taking altogether different directions. On the Indian side, there is no river named 'Sarayu' anywhere near the present Ghaggar-Hakra or the ancient Sarasvatī. But in Afghanistan the existence of two rivers named 'Sarayu' and 'Sarasvatī', in close proximity of one another, has been documented since earliest times and can still be seen in the drainage configuration of the country today. In the *Avesta*, these two rivers, Haroyu and Haraxvaity, are frequently named simultaneously. Similarly, in Achaemenian inscriptions, 'Haroiva' and 'Harauti' are also named one after another. The Greeks, who like the Persians ruled this territory for quite some time, also describe the two rivers, one after another, the Aria and the Arachosia.

The river Sarayu of the *Ṛgveda* (Avestan Haroyu, Achaemenian Haroiva) is at present represented by the Harirud. The Harirud rises in the Hindu Kush mountains near Kabul and runs from east to west for a distance of 400 km. Thereafter, it turns north to form the border between Iran and Afghanistan and disappears in the sandy marshes after covering another 600 km. in this direction. The river Sarasvatī (Avestan Haraxvaity), Achaemenian Harauti is today represented by the Argandab, which rises in the northern mountains and travels in a southerly direction to meet the Helmand, after covering a distance of 500 km. The events recounted in the few passages of the *Ṛgveda* may signify raging hegemonic conflicts between neighbouring chiefdoms, sometime during the second millennium BC. Accordingly, Citra or Citraratha, who ruled the Sarasvatī Valley may have extended his authority to the neighbouring region of the Sarayu Valley. This attracted the wrath of certain other chiefs who finally eliminated Citra and Arṇa on the banks of the Harirud.

Notes

1. R.N. Nandi, *An Outline of the Aryan Civilization*, New Delhi: Manohar, 2017, chapter 5.
2. A. Sarkar et al., 'Oxygen Isotope in Archaeological Bioapatities from India: Implications to Climate Change and Decline of Bronze Age Harappan Civilization', *Nature.Com*, Scientific Reports 6, no. 26555, 2016.
3. Ibid.
4. M.R. Mughal, 'The Consequences of River Changes for the Harappan Settlements in Cholistan', *Eastern Anthropologist*, vol. 45, nos. 1 and 2, 1992, pp. 105–16.
5. A. Hillebrandt, *Vedische Mythologie*, 3 vols., 1st edn., Breslau, 1891, 1899, 1902; tr. (from German) S.R. Sarma, repr., Delhi: Motilal Banarsidass, 1990, vol. 1, p. 343.
6. Nandi, *An Outline of the Aryan Civilization*.

7

Animals in Art and Literature

THE GRADUAL REPLACEMENT of a warm and humid climate by a hyper-arid climatic regime around late third millennium BC badly affected the biological composition of the area. The archaeological documentation of faunal remains in the Greater Indus Valley during the third millennium BC and earlier show that the area was a natural habitat for several animal species that are no longer found in the region. The most important among these animals are the tiger, the elephant and the rhinoceros. Except for the elephant, the other two animals are obstinately wild. Even the domestication of the elephant may have been a difficult proposition and therefore avoidable.

Elephant, Tiger and Rhinoceros

If the Harappan glyptic art is any indication, all the three animals were found in large numbers in the Greater Indus Valley at least till the end of the third millennium BC. Significantly, out of 3,000-odd specimens of glyptic art, nearly half as many relate to the representation of different animals, the most popular being the unicorn and the humped bull. The elephant is represented on 55 items, the rhinoceros on 39 specimens and the tiger on 21 pieces of glyptic art. Five of these 21 representations are depicted with a horn. As already stated elsewhere[1] the representations of the animal signify some sort of message or idea in the Harappan sign system. The message may be variable where the depiction of the same animal is slightly different. Other animals depicted on the Harappan seals include the buffalo, the goat, the hare with the bush, the hare without the bush, besides the humped bull and the unicorn. The unicorn, which appears to have been an imaginary creature, accounts for the largest number of representations.

A word of caution is necessary before attempting any correlation of the actual faunal composition during the third millennium BC and the representation of animals in Harappan glyptic art. There is no precise periodization of these representations. No one knows for sure when these representations began to appear, which ones and how many, or when these representations ceased to appear in the glyptic art. By periodization, we mean not the archaeological strata of different sites but actual dates, which do not vary beyond a period of fifty years on either side. Perhaps such a determination is not achievable at present, given the highly flexible C14 dates. The second point that needs stressing here is that non-representation of certain animals is not the evidence of their non-existence. Similarly, the glyptic representation of certain animals is also no indication of their being coeval in time with the people of Harappan cities. Many of these may have been already on the verge of extinction and many others may have come down the ancestral memory lane.

The gradual disappearance of certain animals in the wake of a hyper-arid episode may also have provided a measure of sanctification to the concerned representation, perhaps a wish against their regression. Third, the representations were part of a sign system and each category of representation conveyed a particular message. For instance, the hare with the bush conveyed one message and the hare without the bush conveyed another. The rhinoceros conveyed one message and a pair of rhinoceros another. Elephants and tigers conveyed separate messages, whereas the horned elephant and the horned tiger conveyed quite different messages. Evidently, the representations were selective and message specific. The non-representation of a large number of animals has, therefore, to be considered in the light of such selectivity. There are no representations of dogs, rodents, reptiles and birds on the Harappan seals. This does not mean that they were absent in the Greater Indus Valley during the third millennium BC.

Recent discoveries of elephant fossils from the Kashmir Valley are significant inasmuch as the elephant is unused to the dizzy altitudes of the Pir Panjal range. The latest elephant fossil dates back to 50,000 years BC, when the Pir Panjal range must have been a sub-montane or foothills forest in the outlying areas. The Himalayas are said to be rising continuously ever since their appearance on the continent. They are still doing so at the rate of one inch every year. The sub-montane or foothills forest among the Himalayas may have been the habitat of the tiger, the elephant and the rhinoceros during the Early Pleistocene period. Perhaps, much before the beginning of the third millennium BC, the higher elevation of these forests had driven away most of these animals towards the east and north-east. Conditions were further aggravated by the onset of a hyper-arid episode from the fourth millennium BC. No wonder that the few specimens that remained in the area drew the special attention of the Harappan peoples, who were trying to perpetuate their existence through their representations of a sign system.

The likely gaps in the archaeological reconstruction of the faunal record may also apply to the earliest literary record of South Asia. For instance, there are neither any representations of the lion and the wolf in the Harappan sign system nor have their bones been identified in the excavations. However, both these animals are fairly prominent in the *Ṛgveda*. Does this automatically suggest that the wolf and the lion did not form part of Harappan fauna? The wolf belongs to the canine species with no particular habitat preferences and can, therefore, exist even in areas with a thin vegetation cover of grass and shrubs, such as the Rajasthan desert after 2000 BC. Similarly, the absence of any mention of the tiger or the rhinoceros need not automatically suggest that the Aryas of the *Ṛgveda* were unfamiliar with these animals.

A good look at the later Vedic text will show that references to the tiger are extremely meagre in these sources. The *Atharvaveda* mentions the terms *Dvipin* and *Vyāghra* once each. In another text the term *Śārdula* is mentioned once. However, there are no references to the rhinoceros till the post-Vedic period. The term *Khaḍgaḥ* is mentioned once each in the *Maitrāyaṇī Śrauta Sūtra* and the *Śānkhyāyana Śrauta Sūtra*. This is quite surprising, since most scholars argue that during the Later Vedic period, the Vedic speakers had penetrated the warm and humid zones on the east and the south.

As for the elephant, the term *Hastin* figures in about seven passages of the *Ṛgveda*, although only two of these can be identified as representative of the pachyderm. The precise term is not *Hastin*, but *Hastīmṛga*, meaning the animal with a hand. One of these two passages referred to elephants ravaging the trees in different forests. In all likelihood, the elephant was still surviving in the forest of the outlying areas towards the north, the east and the south. After all, this is the area towards which population shifts were taking place from the close of the third millennium BC.

The Lion

The lion, which is the second largest felidae after the tiger, finds no representation on the Harappan seals, although it is quite prominent in the bardic descriptions. The lion prefers almost the same habitat as the tiger and, therefore, there is no reason for its omission from the Harappan sign system. The male of the species with the thick beautiful mane around its neck appears majestic and for that reason should have been an automatic item of the sign system. Compared to this, the lion or *siṃha* occurs in nearly twenty passages of the *Ṛgveda*. The one characteristic of the lion which seems to have appealed to the bardic mind was its roar. The roar of the lion is used as a simile in eulogizing several divinities like Indra and the Marūts. These compositions may relate to the bardic composers, who were familiar with the warm and humid climate in the neighbouring Gujarat region in the south and the forests of eastern and south-eastern Haryana. Even today, the most important sanctuary of the lion is the Gir forest in Gujarat.

The lion is a lethargic felidae and depends heavily on the catches made by the lioness. This lethargy may have prevented the animal from travelling very far in search of a favourable habitat and, accordingly, it did not proceed beyond the forest ranges of Gujarat, Haryana and Rajasthan. The lion, zoologically recognized as *Panthera Leo*, is said to have seven sub-species, three of which are endangered and three already extinct. *Panthera Leo Persica*, or the Indian lion, which is today confined to the Gir sanctuary of Gujarat, is one of these endangered sub-species. The Gir forest was probably a natural habitat of the Indian lion since prehistoric times, the earliest fossil the world over dating back to 15000 BC.

An important reason for the decrease in the number of animals may also have been related to fights for male hegemony in the course of which the dominant male kills and even devours the cubs sired by the humbled male. Apart from this, the males are not enterprising unlike their female counterparts, and they depend heavily on the catches made by the lioness. A lion's own attempt to catch a prey has only 30 per cent success. When catches fail, the lion does not make another attempt but looks to snatch prey from the jaws of other predators. All these factors may have compounded the marginalization and subsequent endangerment of the animal.

The Horse

As for the horse, the bones of the animal or the absence of them has long been a source of controversy among archaeologists leading to divergent opinions. The representation of the animal in the Harappan glyptic art and the discovery of equidae bones from different parts of the Greater Indus Valley are focal points of a raging debate as to whether these refer to the horse (*Equus caballus*), the onager (*Equus hemionus*) or the ass (*Equus asinus*). There is no doubt that the onager and the ass were domesticated by the Harappans from very early times, whereas the domestication of horse was confined to certain regions like Gujarat, which is said to be a natural habitat of the equidae family. A good survey of equidae bones in the Harappan context is worth reproducing here.[2]

There are claims for the presence of the horse (*Equus caballus*) at Harappa,[3] Ropar,[4] Mohenjo-daro[5] and Kalibangan.[6] Horse remains have been reported from Bronze Age sites in Gujarat and Surkotada in Kutch,[7] Lothal,[8] Malvan[9] and Kanewal.[10]

The bones of *Equus hemionus* have been found at Rojdi[11] and Surkotada.[12] A 'domestic ass' has been identified in a preliminary report for Kalibangan, which may be *Equus hemionus*.[13] Archaeologists have also identified the ass (*Equus asinus*) and the horse (*Equus caballus*) at Rana Ghundai in northern Baluchistan.[14] In a slightly later context, the horse and ass have been identified at Pirak, a site of the second millennium BC, very close to Mehrgarh and Nausharo.[15] There are also terracotta figurines of an equid which are said to be a reasonably convincing rendering of *Equus caballus*.[16]

The onager (*Equus hemionus*) and horse (*Equus caballus*) are closely related and their osteological remains are not easily distinguished.[17] Differences are present, but it requires skill and good comparative material to determine them. The evidence from terracotta figurines is even more difficult to be used in distinguishing the ass from the horse. Because the onager is native to the Greater Indus Region, there is a reasonable certainty that some, perhaps all, of the bones and teeth found so far at archaeological sites of the Indus Age are from this animal. The onager was part of their environment and it is not surprising that the Harappans made terracotta figurines of them.[18]

Finding the remains of *Equus caballus* in northern and southern Afghanistan, or Seistan, for example, would strengthen the case for horses at Mohenjo-daro and Surkotada.[19] One thing that seems clear is that the Harappans could not have domesticated this animal because its wild progenitor was not part of their environment.

The case is not the same with the *Equus przewalskii.* This animal is reliably believed to be the domesticated form of a smaller animal known as the tarpan or przewalski's horse, *Equus przewalskii*, which is at home to the north of the Indus region in Chinese Turkistan, Mongolia, Central Asia, the Trans-Caspian and Ukraine in the west. It is not native to the Greater Indus Region. The time and place for the domestication of the true horse (*Equus caballus*) is not known.

However, Possehl seems a little undecided about the domestication of *Equus caballus* by the Harappans when he either states on his own or quotes approvingly from other specialists to say that, 'there are also terracotta figurines of an equid that is a reasonably convincing rendering of *Equus caballus*',[20] that 'horse remains have been reported from Bronze Age sites in Gujarat and from Surkotada in Kutch,[21] Lothal[22] and Kanewal',[23] that 'Gujarat is one of the few places in the subcontinent where horses can be successfully bred' and that their appearance in Gujarat and Kutch at this early date is certainly in keeping with this historical observation.

Some observation of the *Equus hemionus* and its correlation with literary information would at once show that in the third millennium BC context of north-western South Asia, the presence or absence of *Equus caballus* is of little consequence. The onager, which provides plentiful good meat, functions efficiently as pack animal or draft animal and runs even faster than the horse,[24] could very well represent the horse in north-western South Asia during the third millennium BC. A shy animal, slightly shorter in height than the horse, the onager is remarkable for its speed and at times it can leave the fleetest horse behind.[25] In the earliest literary records, it is the distinctive reddish-brown colour that is associated with the terms meaning a horse. The *Ṛgveda*, which is the earliest literary record of north-western South Asia, has several terms meaning a horse. The more important of these are *Aśva, Tura, Ḥayah, Hari, Arvat* and *Vāji.* Of these, the term *Aśva* occurs 368 times in the text, including a hundred compounds. The term may derive from √*aś* meaning 'to reach, visit, arrive', but more appropriately from 'Aśu', which is also derived from √*aś*, but means 'fast, quick'. 'Āśu' figures 86 times in the *Ṛgveda* in the sense of quick or fast, but in several passages, it means the horse itself. *Tura* meaning 'quick, powerful, prompt', appears 49 times in the *Ṛgveda* and on several occasions in the sense of a horse. *Haya* from √*hi*, meaning 'send forth, stimulate', is much less recurrent in the text, appearing in five passages in the sense of a horse. *Hari*, which signifies several colours, like brown, yellow, tawny, pale, and appears nearly 150 times in the text, also means a horse in a few passages. *Arvat* meaning 'running, hasting, a courser', appears 85 times, mostly in the sense of the horse. *Vāji* is nominative singular of the term *Vāja*, which means several completely different things like 'energy or strength', 'a contest or battle', 'booty, gain or reward' and 'a swift horse', appears nearly 200 times in the text. It may have been applied to the horse, since the animal was a symbol of strength and instrumental in fighting a battle or capturing booty. This vocabulary of the horse underlines that the animal was the symbol of strength and swiftness.

The pre-eminence of the onager and the supposed absence of the horse in the Harappan context of the third millennium BC may, however, create certain problems for scholars trying to reconstruct social contexts on the basis of language. In one study, by Southworth, the Dravidian dialect spoken in South Asia is divided into five time-frames termed 'proto-Dravidian-0', 'proto-Dravidian-1', 'proto-Dravidian-2', 'proto-Dravidian-3' and 'proto-Dravidian-4'.[26] According to Southworth, proto-Dravidian-0, which represented the earliest Dravidian speakers of South Asia, has a word for the horse. This is considered to be a strong suggestion that the people who spoke this language lived in a region other than peninsular India. The suggestion is based on the observation of Burrow,[27] who notes the existence of a word for the horse, which is found only in Tamil, *ivuli*, and Brahui, *(h)ullī*.[28] A word of caution is necessary here since clearly there is a mix-up. Burrow may have examined the word *ivuli* or *(h)ullī* in his 1972 article, but there is no mention of these terms in the dictionary brought out by him in 1960. The *Dravidian Etymological Dictionary* does not have any term for 'horse'. Instead, it has *utakku* in Tamil, meaning 'to be fitted to the string of the bow', and *ulakku* in Malayalam, meaning 'catch, latching, notch, obstruction'. There is no trace of the words *ivuli* or *(h)ullī* either in the separate lists of Dravidian dialects appended to the book. The Tamil *ullī*, meaning 'onion, garlic', and Kannada *ulli*, meaning 'in this intermediate place', also do not help. There is another mix-up in relation to the Tamil term for 'horse'—*kutirai*.[29] Considering the pre-eminence of the onager in north-western South Asia, the *ivuli* or *(h)ullī* may be the same as *Equus hemionus*, which is native to South Asia, rather than the domesticated horse, *Equus caballus*, which was not introduced into South Asia until after 2000 BC.[30] Similarly, quoting McAlpin approvingly, Southworth states that the *Dravidian* word for the domesticated horse, proto-Dravidian-3 *kutirai* (DED 1711), is a loan from Elamite.[31] However, DED 1711 has nothing to do with the horse though Tamil *kotu ka*, *kotu ki*, Malayalam *kotu ka*, Kannada *kodu*, all meaning, 'to shrink or shiver with cold', is phonemically closer to Sanskrit, *ghoṭaka*, meaning 'horse'. One needs to look for *kutirai* DED 1423, which has Tamil *kutirai*, meaning 'horse'; Malayalam *kutira*, meaning 'horse, cavalry'; Kota *kudire*, *kudure*, *kudare*, meaning 'horse'; Kodagu *kudire*; Tulu *tudure*; Telugu *kudira*, *kudaramu*, *gurramu*; Kolami *gurram*; Naiki *ghurram*; Konda *gurram*; Pali *gurrol*. Whether, a loan from Elamite or not, *kutirai* may have devolved into the most familiar term *ghoda* in Hindi, *khor* in Persian, *ghoṭāh* in Sanskrti and horse in English. The presence of alveolar in Telugu *gurramu*, Konda *gurram* and Pali *gurrol*, seems only one step from the cerebral '*ḍ*' in *ghora* or *ghorā*. In the English term 'horse', the absence of a vowel between consonants 'r' and 's', also tends to cerebralize and, accordingly, horse would be phonetically quite close to *ghoḍā* or *ghoṭā*.

The Horse Riders

The presence of *Equus caballus* within a certain community calls for determining the possible uses to which the animal may have been put. There are examples in which people learnt to domesticate the horse, but used it for diet and ritual purposes, as in the case of European Steppe people during 5000 BC. There are other examples in which the horse was regularly bitted and ridden, probably to hunt wild horses as at Botai, east of the Urals, between 3500 and 3000 BC.[32] The importance of horse and horse-riding at this Kazakh site is evident from the fact that 90 per cent of animal bones recovered from this site are those of horses. The most important evidence of the bridling or bitting of horses is bit wear in the form of a significant bevel or slope on the front or mesial corner of the lower second premolars.[33] The bevelling is caused as the bridled or bitted horse chews up the bit in the course of riding, which increases the bevel or slope in the lower second premolars either on one side or both, depending on the manner in which the rider controlled the horse. Bits could be made from organic materials, like hemp, horse hair, leather and bone, besides metal. The metal bit causes the maximum damage to the dental pathology of the equid. Among the organic bits, it is the hemp and the bone that causes maximum increase in the bevelling of the lower second premolars of horses, whereas bits made of leather and horse hair almost do not affect the dental pathology of the animal.

In the Harappan context, there is no dearth of equid bones throughout the Greater Indus Valley, but there are no representations of horse-riders in Harappan glyptic art. No studies of equid dental pathology from the area are still forthcoming, to indicate whether the animal, horse or onager was controlled by the rider with the help of bits of some sort. In case, the bits were made from horse hair, leather or some similar soft materials, the possibility of increased bevelling in the lower second premolars of the equid could be difficult to come by. Bits can be altogether out of reckoning in the event of the rider controlling the equid with reins passing through the nostrils of the animal. This is precisely what appears in one passage of the

Ṛgveda (5.61.2) which refers to *Nasoyamaḥ* or the rope passing through the nostril of the horse. *Nasoyamaḥ* is understood by Sāyaṇ as the part of the reins that passes through the nostrils of the horse and prevents it from running away. The passage also refers to *Abhiṣu*, or the whip, which actually was the part of the reins held by the rider and used to strike the animal on its neck whenever required. Probably the saddle was also in use, as can be seen from the mention of *Pṛṣṭhe Sadaḥ* (5.61.2). This must have been a thick sitting pad with nooses of rope hanging on either side for holding fast the feet of the rider. The image of the rider that emerges from this description would be of a person who held the reins with one hand and some weapon in the other. For goading the horse to move on, the rider used to strike the thigh of the horse with his feet ('Jaghane codah', 5.61.3). The expression is formed by locative *Jaghane* and the √*cud*, meaning 'to motivate, to impel, to force, to activate, to send' and so on.

Notes

1. R.N. Nandi, *An Outline of the Aryan Civilization*, New Delhi: Manohar, 2017, chapter 12.
2. G.L. Possehl, *Indus Age: The Beginnings*, New Delhi and Calcutta: Oxford and IBH, 1999, p. 186.
3. Baini Prashad, *Animal Remains from Harappa: Memoirs of the Archaeological Survey of India*, Delhi: Archaeological Survey of India, 1936, p. 51; Bhola Nath, 'Remains of the Horse and Indian Elephant from the Pre-historic Site of Harappa (West Pakistan)', *Proceedings of the First All-India Congress of Zoology, 1959: Part 2, Scientific Papers*, Calcutta: The Zoological Society of India, 1962, pp. 1–14.
4. Bhola Nath, 'Animal Remains from Rupar and Bara Sites,

Ambala District, East Punjab', *Indian Museum Bulletin*, vol. 3, nos. 1 and 2, 1968, pp. 69–115.

5. R.B. Seymour-Sewell and B.S. Guha, 'Zoological Remains', in *Mohenjo-daro and the Indus Civilization*, ed. John Marshall, vol. 3, London: Arthur Probsthain, 1931, pp. 649–73.
6. A.K. Sharma, 'Animal Bone Remains', in *Excavation at Surkotada 1971–2 and Exploration in Kutch*, ed. J.P. Joshi, New Delhi: Archaeological Survey of India, 1990, pp. 372–83.
7. Sharma, 'Animal Bone Remains'; S. Bokonyi, 'Horse Remains from the Prehistoric Site of Surkotada, Kutch, Late 3rd Millennium B.C.', *South Asian Studies*, vol. 13, no. 1, 1997, pp. 297–307.
8. Bhola Nath and G.V.S. Rao, 'Animal Remains from the Lothal Excavations', in S.R. Rao, *Lothal: A Harappan Port Town, 1955-62, Memoirs of the Archaeological Survey of India*, no. 78, vol. 2, 1985, pp. 636–50.
9. Sharma, 'Animal Bone Remains'.
10. D.R. Sahni, *Excavations at Harappa*, Annual Progress Report of the Superintendent, Hindu and Buddhist Monuments, Northern Circle, for the Year Ending 31st March 1921, Lahore: Civil and Military Gazette Press, 1920–1, 8.26.
11. V.S. Kane, 'Animal Remains from Rojdi', in *Harappan Civilization and Rojdi*, ed. G.L. Possehl and M.H. Raval, Delhi: Oxford and IBH, 1989, p. 183.
12. Sharma, 'Animal Bone Remains'.
13. A. Ghosh, ed., *Indian Archaeology 1964–65, A Review*, Report of the Archaeological Survey of India, Delhi: Archaeological Survey of India, 1969, p. 38.
14. B.S. Guha and B.K. Chatterjee, 'Report on Skeletal Remains', Part II of 'A Chalcolithic Site in Northern Baluchistan' by E.J. Ross, *Journal of Near Eastern Studies*, vol. 5, no. 4, 1946, pp. 315–16.

15. R.H. Meadow, 'A Preliminary Report on the Faunal Remains from Pirak', in *Fouilles de Pirak*, ed. J.-F. Jarrige and M. Santoni, vol. 1, Publications de la Commission des Fouilles Archaeologiques. Fouilles du Pakistan, no. 2, Paris: Diffusion De Boccard, 1979.
16. J.-F. Enault, *Fouilles de Pirak*, vol. 2, Publications de la Commission des Fouilles Archaeologique, Fouilles du Pakistan, no. 2, Paris: Diffusion De Boccard, 1979.
17. Possehl, *Indus Age.*
18. Ibid.
19. Ibid.
20. Enault, *Fouilles de Pirak*, vol. 2.
21. Sharma, 'Animal Bone Remains'; Bokonyi, 'Horse Remains from the Prehistoric Site of Surkotada'.
22. Nath and Rao, 'Animal Remains from the Lothal Excavations'; Sharma, 'Animal Bone Remains'.
23. Sahni, *Excavations at Harappa.*
24. M. Elphinstone, *An Account of the Kingdom of Caubul and its Dependencies in Persia, Tartary and India: Comprising a View of the Afghaun Nation and a History of Dooraunee Monarchy*, vol. 2, London: Longman, Hurst and Ree, Orm and Brown and John Murray, 1819.
25. Ibid.
26. F.C. Southworth, 'Reconstructing Social Context from Language: Indo-Aryan and Dravidian Prehistory', in *Indo-Aryans of Ancient South Asia: Language Material Culture and Ethnicity*, ed. G. Erdosy, Berlin and New York: Walter de Gruyter, 1995; repr., New Delhi: Munshiram Manoharlal, 1995, p. 268n13.
27. T. Burrow, 'The Primitive Dravidian Word for the Horse', *International Journal of Dravidian Linguistics*, vol. 1, 1972, pp. 18–25.

28. T. Burrow and M.B. Emeneau, *A Dravidian Etymological Dictionary*, Amen House, London: Oxford University Press, 1960, p. 605.
29. Ibid.
30. Southworth, 'Reconstructing Social Context from Language'.
31. Ibid.
32. A.P. Derevyanko and D. Dorj, 'Neolithic Tribes in Northern Parts of Central Asia', in *History of Civilizations of Central Asia*, vol. 1, Paris: UNESCO, 1992; repr., 1st Indian edn., Delhi: Motilal Banarsidaas, 1999, p. 185.
33. D.W. Anthony and D.R. Brown, 'Eneolithic Horse Exploitation in the Eurasian Steppes: Diet, Ritual and Riding', *Antiquity*, vol. 74, no. 283, March 2000, pp. 75–86.

Bibliography

Anthony, D.W. and D.R. Brown, 'Eneolithic Horse Exploitation in the Eurasian Steppes: Diet, Ritual and Riding', *Antiquity*, vol. 74, no. 283, March 2000, pp. 75–86.

Arnold, E.V, *Vedic Metre in its Historical Development*, 1st edn., Cambridge: Cambridge University Press, 1905; repr., Delhi: Motilal Banarsidass, 1967.

Bokonyi, S., 'Horse Remains from the Prehistoric Site of Surkotada, Kutch, Late 3rd Millennium B.C.', *South Asian Studies*, vol. 13, no. 1, pp. 297–307.

Boone, E.H. and W.D. Mignolo, eds., *Writing Without Words: Alternative Literacies in Mesoamerica and the Andes*, Durham, North Carolina: Duke University Press, 1994.

Boyce, M., 'Avestan People', in *Encyclopaedia Iranica*, ed. Y. Ehsan, vol. III, London and New York: Routledge & Kegan Paul, 1989.

Bresinsky, A. and H. Besl, *Giftpilze: Ein Handbuch für Apotheker Ärtzte und Biologen*, Stuttgart: Wissenschaftliche Verlagsgesellschaft, 1985.

Burrow, T., *The Sanskrit Language*, 1st edn., London: Faber, 1955, rev. edn., London: Faber, 1970.

———, 'The Primitive Dravidian Word for the Horse', *International Journal of Dravidian Linguistics*, vol. 1, 1972, pp. 18–25.

Burrow, T. and M.B. Emeneau, *A Dravidian Etymological Dictionary*, Amen House, London: Oxford University Press, 1960.

Chen, K.K. and C.F. Smith, 'Ephedrine and Related Substances', *Medicine*, vol. 9, 1930, pp. 1–117.

Dani, A.H. and B.K. Thapar, 'The Indus Civilization', in *History of Civilizations of Central Asia*, ed. A.H. Dani and V.M. Masson, vol. 1, Paris: UNESCO, 1992; repr., 1st Indian edn., Delhi: Motilal Banarsidass, 1999.

Derevyanko, A.P. and D. Dorj, 'Neolithic Tribes in Northern Parts of Central Asia', in *History of Civilizations of Central Asia*, ed. A.H. Dani and V.M. Masson, vol. 1, Paris: UNESCO, 1992; repr., 1st Indian edn., Delhi: Motilal Banarsidass, 1999.

Deshpande, M.M., *Sanskrit and Prakrit: Sociolinguistic Issues*, Delhi: Motilal Banarsidass, 1993.

Dhavalikar, M. and S. Atre, 'The Fire Cult and Virgin Sacrifice: Some Harappan Rituals', in *Old Problems and New Perspectives in the Archaeology of South Asia, Wisconsin Archaeology Reports*, ed. J.M. Kenoyer, vol. 2, Department of Anthropology, Madison: Wisconsin University Press, 1989, pp. 193–207.

Elphinstone, M., *An Account of the Kingdom of Caubul and its Dependencies in Persia, Tartary and India: Comprising a view of the Afghaun Nation and a History of Dooraunee Monarchy*, vol. 2, London: Longman, Hurst and Ree, Orm and Brown and John Murray, 1819.

Emeneau, M.B., *Brahui and Dravidian Comparative Grammar*, Berkeley: University of California Press, 1962.

Enault, J.-F., *Fouilles de Pirak*, vol. 2, Paris: Publications de la Commission des Fouilles Archaeologique, Fouilles du Pakistan, no. 2, Paris: Diffusion De Boccard, 1979

Erdosy, G., 'Ethnicity in the *Rigveda* and its Bearing on the Problem of Indo-European Origins', *South Asian Studies*, vol. 5, no. 1, 1989, pp. 35–47.

Falk, H., 'Soma I and II', *Bulletin of the School of Oriental and African Studies*, vol. 52, pp. 77–90.

Farmer, S., J.B. Henderson and M. Witzel, eds., 'Neurobiology, Layered Text and Correlative Cosmologies: A Cross-cultural Framework for Pre-modern History', *Bulletin of the Museum of Far Eastern Antiquities*, vol. 72, 2002, pp. 48–89.

Farmer, S., R. Sproat and M. Witzel, 'The Collapse of the Indus-Script Thesis: The Myth of a Literate Harappan Civilization', *Electronic Journal of Vedic Studies*, vol. 11, no. 2, 13 December 2004, pp. 19–57.

Flattery, D.S. and M. Schwartz, *Haoma and Harmaline: The Botanical Identity of the Indo-Iranian Sacred Hallucinogen 'Soma' and its Legacy in Religion, Language and Middle Eastern Folklore*, Berkeley: University of California Press, 1989.

Fujiwara, H., M.R. Mughal, A. Sasaki and T. Matano, 'Rice and Ragi at Harappa: Preliminary Results by Plant Opal Analysis', *Pakistan Archaeology*, vol. 27, 1992, pp.129–42, 369–80, repr., in *The Decline and Fall of the Indus Civilization*, ed. N. Lahiri, New Delhi: Permanent Black, 2000.

Fuller, D.Q. and E.C. Harvey, 'The Archaeobotany of Indian Pulses: Identification, Processing and Evidence for Cultivation', *Environmental Archaeology*, vol. 11, no. 2, 2006, pp. 219–46.

Ghosh, A., ed., *Indian Archaeology 1964–65: A Review*, Report of the Archaeological Survey of India, Delhi: Archaeological Survey of India, 1969.

———, ed., *An Encyclopaedia of Indian Archaeology*, vol. 1, Indian Council of Historical Research, New Delhi: Munshiram Manoharlal, 1989.

Gimbutas, M., 'The Neolithic, Chalcolithic and Copper Ages in the North Pontic Area', in *The Prehistory of Eastern Europe Part 1: Mesolithic, Neolithic and Copper Age Cultures in Russia and the*

Baltic Area, American School of Prehistory Research, Peabody Museum, Harvard University, Bulletin No. 20, Cambridge, Massachusetts: Peabody Museum, 1956.

Good, I.L., J.M. Kenoyer and R.H. Meadow, 'New Evidence for Early Silk in the Indus Civilization', *Archaeometry*, vol. 51, no. 3, 2009, pp. 457–66.

Guha, B.S. and B.K. Chatterjee, 'Report on Skeletal Remains', Part II of 'A Chalcolithic Site in Northern Baluchistan' by E.J. Ross, *Journal of Near Eastern Studies*, vol. 5, no. 4, 1946, pp. 315–16.

Hegenauer, R., *Chemotaxonomie der Pflanzen*, vol. 1, Basel: Birkhauser Verlag, 1986.

Hillebrandt, A., *Vedische Mythologie*, 3 vols., 1st edn., Breslau, 1891, 1899, 1902; tr. (from German) S.R. Sarma, repr., Delhi: Motilal Banarsidass, 1990.

Hoffmann K., 'Avesthan Language', in *Encyclopaedia Iranica*, ed. Y. Ehsan, vol. III, London and New York: Routledge and Kegan Paul, 1989, pp. 47–62.

Kane, V.S., 'Animal Remains from Rojdi', in *Harappan Civilization and Rojdi*, ed. G.L. Possehl and M.H. Raval, Delhi: Oxford and IBH, 1989.

Keith, A.B., *Rigveda Brahmanas: The Aitareya and Kauṣītaki Brāhmaṇas of the Rigveda*, 1st edn., Cambridge, Mass.: Harvard University Press, 1920; repr., Delhi: Motilal Banarsidass, 1998.

Kuiper, F.B.J., *Aryans in the Ṛgveda*, Amsterdam-Atlanta: Rodopi, 1991.

Kussov, S., '"White Rooms" in the Temples of Margiana', *New Studies in Bronze Age Margiana, Information Bulletin of the International Association for the Study of the Cultures of Central Asia*, vol. 19, ed. F. Hiebert, Moscow: Nauka, 1993, pp. 128–35.

Martens, P., *Les Gnetophytes*, vol. 2, Handbuch der Pflanzenanatomie XII, Berlin: Gebruder Bomtraeger, 1971.

Masson, V.M., 'The Decline of the Bronze Age Civilization and Movements of the Tribes', in *History of Civilizations of Central Asia*, ed. A.H. Dani and V.M. Masson, vol. 1, Paris: UNESCO,

1992; repr., 1st Indian edn., Delhi: Motilal Banarsidass, 1999, pp. 337–56.

———, 'The Bronze Age in Khorasan and Transoxania', in *History of Civilizations of Central Asia*, ed. A.H. Dani and V.M. Masson, vol. l, Paris: UNESCO, 1992; repr., 1st Indian edn., Delhi: Motilal Banarsidass, 1999.

McAlpine, D.W., 'Towards Proto-Elemo-Dravidian', *Language*, vol. 50, 1974, pp. 89–101.

McIntosh, J.R., *The Ancient Indus Valley: New Perspectives*, Santa Barbara, California: ABC-CLIO, 2008.

Meadow, R. H., 'A Preliminary Report on the Faunal Remains from Pirak', in J.-F. Jarrige and M. Santoni, eds., *Fouilles de Pirak*, vol. 1, Publications de la Commission des Fouilles Archaeologiques. Fouilles du Pakistan, no. 2, Paris: Diffusion De Boccard, 1979.

Meadow, R.H. and J.M. Kenoyer, 'Harappa Excavations 1993: The City Wall and Inscribed Materials', in *South Asian Archaeology, 1993*, ed. A. Parpola and K. Koskikallio, Helsinki: Suomalainen Tiedeakatemia, 1994.

Mughal, M.R., 'The Consequences of River Changes for the Harappan Settlements in Cholistan', *Eastern Anthropologist*, vol. 45, nos. 1 and 2, 1992.

Nandi, R.N., *Aryans Revisited*, New Delhi: Munshiram Manoharlal, 2001.

———, *Ideology and Environment: Situating the Origin of Vedic Culture*, Delhi: Akaar, 2009.

———, *An Outline of the Aryan Civilization*, New Delhi: Manohar, 2017.

Nath, Bhola, 'Remains of the Horse and Indian Elephant from the Pre-historic Site of Harappa (West Pakistan)', *Proceedings of the First All-India Congress of Zoology 1959: Part 2, Scientific Papers*, Calcutta: The Zoological Society of India, 1962, pp. 1–14.

———, 'Animal Remains from Rupar and Bara Sites, Ambala District, East Punjab', *Indian Museum Bulletin*, vol. 3, nos. 1 and 2, 1968, pp. 69–115.

Nath, Bhola and G.V.S. Rao, 'Animal Remains from the Lothal Excavations', in S.R. Rao, *Lothal: A Harappan Port Town, 1955-62, Memoirs of the Archaeological Survey of India*, no. 78, vol. 2, 1985, pp. 636–50.

Nyberg, H., 'The Problem of the Aryans and the Soma: The Botanical Evidence', in *The Indo-Aryans of Ancient South Asia: Language, Material Culture and Ethnicity*, ed. G. Erdosy, Berlin: Walter de Gruyter and Co., 1995; repr., 1st Indian edn., Delhi: Munshiram Manoharlal, 1997.

Parpola, A., *Deciphering the Indus Script*, 1994; repr., Cambridge: Cambridge University Press, 1997.

———, 'The Problem of the Aryans and the Soma: Textual-linguistic and Archaeological Evidence', in *The Indo-Aryans of Ancient South Asia: Language, Material Culture and Ethnicity*, ed. G. Erdosy, Berlin: Walter de Gruyter and Co., 1995; repr., 1st Indian edn., Delhi: Munshiram Manoharlal, 1997.

Possehl, G.L., *Indus Age: The Beginnings*, New Delhi and Calcutta: Oxford and IBH, 1999.

Prashad, Baini, *Animal Remains from Harappa: Memoirs of the Archaeological Survey of India*, Delhi: Archaeological Survey of India, 1936.

Richter-Ushanas, E., *The Indus Script and the Ṛgveda*, Delhi: Motilal Banarsidass, 1997.

Sahni, D.R., *Excavations at Harappa*, Annual Progress Report of the Superintendent, Hindu and Buddhist Monuments, Northern Circle, for the Year Ending 31st March 1921, Lahore: Civil and Military Gazette Press, 1920–1.

Sarianidi, V.L, 'Southwest Asia: Migrations, the Aryans and Zoroastrians', *Information Bulletin of the International Association for the Study of the Cultures of Central Asia*, vol. 13, 1987, pp. 44–56.

Sarkar, A., A.D. Mukherjee, M.K. Bera, B. Das, N. Juyal, P. Morthekai, R.D. Deshpande, V.S. Shinde and L.S. Rao, 'Oxygen Isotope in Archaeological Bioapatities from India: Implications to Climate

Change and Decline of Bronze Age Harappan Civilization', *Nature.com*, Scientific Reports 6, no. 26555, 2016.

Schultes, R.E. and A. Hofmann, *The Botany and Chemistry of Hallucinogens*, 1995; repr., 2nd edn., Springfield: Charles C. Thomas, 1997.

Seymour-Sewell, R.B. and B.S. Guha, 'Zoological Remains', in *Mohenjo-daro and the Indus Civilization*, ed. John Marshall, vol. 3, London: Arthur Probsthain, 1931, pp. 649–73.

Shaffer, J.G., 'The Indo-Aryan Invasion, Cultural Myth and Archaeological Reality', in *The Biological Anthropology of India, Pakistan, and Nepal*, ed. J.R. Lukacz, New York: Plenum Press, 1984, pp. 77–88.

Shaffer, J.G. and D.A. Lichtenstein, 'The Concepts of "Cultural Tradition" and "Palaeoethnicity" in South Asian Archaeology', in *Indo-Aryans of Ancient South Asia: Language, Material Culture and Ethnicity*, ed. G. Erdosy, Berlin and New York: Walter de Gruyter, 1995; repr., New Delhi: Munshiram Manoharlal, 1995.

Sharma, A.K., 'Animal Bone Remains', in *Excavation at Surkotada 1971–2 and Exploration in Kutch*, ed. J.P. Joshi, New Delhi: Archaeological Survey of India, 1990, pp. 372–83.

Southworth, F.C., 'Reconstructing Social Context from Language: Indo-Aryan and Dravidian Prehistory', in *Indo-Aryans of Ancient South Asia: Language, Material Culture and Ethnicity*, ed. G. Erdosy, Berlin and New York: Walter de Gruyter, 1995; repr., New Delhi: Munshiram Manoharlal, 1995.

Swarup, L., *The Nighantu and the Nirukta*, 1st edn., 1920, 1927; repr., Delhi: Motilal Banarsidass, 1984.

Tikkanen, B., *The Sanskrit Gerund: A Synchronic, Diachronic, and Typological Analysis*, Studia Orientalia 62, Helsinki: Finnish Oriental Society, 1987.

Victoria, S.-K., 'Animal Remains from Rojdi', in *Harappan Civilization and Rojdi*, ed. G.L. Possehl and M.H. Raval, Delhi: Oxford and IBH, 1989.

Wheeler, R.E.M., 'Harappa 1946: The Defences and Cemetery R 37', in *The Indus Civilization*, Cambridge: Cambridge University Press, 1953.

Witzel, M., 'On the Localisation of Vedic Texts and Schools (Materials on Vedic Sakhas, 7)', in *India and the Ancient World: History, Trade and Culture Before* AD *650, P.H.L. Eggermont Jubilee Volume*, ed. G. Pollet, Leuven: Departement Oriëntalistiek, 1987, pp. 173–213.

———, 'Tracing the Vedic Dialects', in *Dialectes dans les litte'ratures indo-aryennes*, ed. Colette Caillat, Paris: Institut de Civilisation Indienne, 1989, pp. 97–264.

———, 'Early Indian History: Linguistic and Textual Parameters', in *The Indo-Aryans of Ancient South Asia, Indian Philology and South Asian Studies 1*, ed. G. Erdosy, Berlin and New York: de Gruyter, 1995, pp. 85–125.

———, 'Rigvedic History: Poets, Chieftains and Polities', in *The Indo-Aryans of Ancient South Asia, Indian Philology and South Asian Studies 1*, ed. G. Erdosy, Berlin and New York: de Gruyter, 1995, pp. 307–52.

———, 'Substrate Languages in Old Indo-Aryan', *Electronic Journal of Vedic Studies*, vol. 5, no. 1, September 1999, p. 96.

Wright, R.P., D.L. Lentz, H.F. Beaubien and C.K. Kimbrough, 'New Evidence for Jute (*Corchorus Capsularis L.*) in the Indus Civilization', *Archaeological and Anthropological Sciences*, vol. 4, no. 2, 2012, pp. 137–43.

Index